Best Wishes
Doreen Potts

A LOOK BACK AT HALSTEAD

A Pictorial History of Halstead

by
Doreen Potts

DEDICATION

To Joyce Willis and Mary Downs

I am dedicating this book to these two ladies, who became very good friends of mine whilst I was in the process of compiling my books. They were next door neighbours, in Parsonage Street, for many years. The help they gave me, with information about Halstead and it's inhabitants, was invaluable and it was a pleasure to have known them. I was deeply saddened in 2001 when they both passed away within a few weeks of each other and therefore never saw this finished publication, a result of their encouragement.

Joyce Lillian Ward was born at 58 Parsonage Street, an old cottage next to the Globe in 1921. She was educated at St Andrews and the Secondary School, leaving at 14 years old to be a weaver at Courtaulds. She married Jack Willis and had one son, Malcolm. She was a quiet lady whose life revolved around her family and friends. The church played a large part in her life where she was once a Sunday School teacher. She enjoyed friends calling in for a chat, especially about local history in which she took a great interest. She died on March 22nd 2001

Evelyn Mary Oxborrow-Smith was born at 4 Garden Terrace, Parsonage Street in 1921. She was also educated at St Andrews, and the Secondary School where she became great friends with Joyce. Mary, as she was known, worked at Doubledays drapery until 1942 when she joined the Women's Land Army. After her discharge five years later she returned to Doubledays, eventually transferring to the grocery. She married Stan Downs in 1954 and continued to work under various owners until her retirement in 1973. Mary died June 2nd 2001.

A LOOK BACK AT HALSTEAD

by
Doreen Potts

Box Mills pre 1882

Morton Mathews, a local artist and schoolmaster painted this picture of how Box Mills looked before April 1882, when the windmill suffered the fate of being blown into the River Colne during a violent storm. It is recorded that "the mill rocked ominously when struck by sudden gusts of wind and forthwith it was blown bodily over, the sails and some of the machinery being deposited into the river." It is probably unique in that it suffered the fate of being "drowned". At the time it was described as being upwards of 100 years old. The watermill, erected before 1730 remained in working order until 1920. These mills were sited within a bend of the river at the lower end of Box Mill Lane.

Published by
Doreen Potts
14 Bourchier Way
Halstead
Essex
CO9 1AY

Printed by
The Lavenham Press Ltd
Arbons House
47 Water Street
Lavenham
Suffolk
CO10 9RN

ISBN 0-9545555-0-3

Further copies are available from the author at

14 Bourchier Way
Halstead
Essex
CO9 1AY

Price £ 9.95 plus £2.00 post and packing.

The photo on the front cover is of
St Andrew's Church, Halstead, taken
at the end of the 1800s.

FOREWORD
By
ADRIAN CORDER-BIRCH, F.Inst.L.Ex., M.I.C.M.,
Patron of Halstead and District Local History Society

I was privileged to be invited by Halstead local historian, Doreen Potts, to write the Foreword for her latest book, 'A Look Back at Halstead'. This excellent book is effectively a sequel to one of Doreen's earlier books 'Halstead's Heritage', which was published as a contribution to Essex Heritage Year in 1989. Since then Doreen has worked very hard to accumulate hundreds of additional photographs of Halstead of which nearly 250 have been carefully selected to illustrate this book. The captions for each illustration have been meticulously researched resulting in this valuable contribution to the numerous publications about the history of the town.

It is exactly one hundred years since the first edition of 'Holman's Halstead' was published in 1902. William Holman, who died in 1730, left a collection of historical notes, which were edited by Rev. T.G. Gibbons and published by W.H. Root. 'Holman's Halstead' together with 'Old and New Halstead' by W.J. Evans, were the only major publications about the history of the town until the recent publications of Halstead and District Local History Society which began in 1979. Since then books written by Percy Bamberger, Dave Osborne, Doreen Potts and others have continued the vital work of recording the history of our town. In the Foreword to the first book in this series in 1979, Sir Ronald Long, then President of Halstead and District Local History Society, wrote "..... presentation of the past will form an invaluable record for the future .....". How true these words were and still are today. Doreen has collated, researched and prepared for us and for future generations another important record of the past. It is important that historical research is published so that information is not lost.

I was very moved when I noticed that Doreen had jointly dedicated this book to Mary Downs. I remember Mary working for Doubledays, which is featured in this book. In fact Mary was initially employed by the last member of the Doubleday family and remained with successive owners for some thirty years. Before moving to Parsonage Street, Mary and her husband had lived in 6 Head Street, before it was converted to offices. These are a few threads in the rich tapestry of our history.

This book truly records all aspects of the town's history from country crafts to major industries, small cottages to mansions, the churches and chapels, schools and street scenes. The residents are also included, with organizations and some of the characters remembered in the town. I am sure that all readers will be grateful to Doreen for the diversity and detail in this well illustrated book, which I commend to you.

Adrian Corder-Birch
Halstead,
Essex. 12th December 2002

AUTHOR'S PREFACE AND ACKNOWLEDGEMENTS

In 1837, Bernard Barton, a Quaker poet wrote to a friend describing Halstead - "The town, a quiet little place about 13 miles sideways of Colchester, was one in which, during 8 years, I saw little or no change. Thirty-one years later I walked here as if in a dream. The names over the shops were changed, the people were not the same, the houses, or most of them were altered. The old Market Place, a piece of rude and simple architecture, which looked as if it might have grown there in the reign of Queen Elizabeth and stood just opposite our shop door; it's place supplied by a pyramidal obelisk bearing 3 gas lamps, gas a thing the good folks there, I will answer for it had scarce heard of 31 years ago. Out on such new-fangled innovations! Had I been apprenticed in London I should have thought nothing of it, but in a little obscure place like Halstead, a spot where all seemed changeless during my 8 years sojourn, I was fairly posed."

Bernard Barton was born in Carlisle in 1784, orphaned at seven years of age, then sent to a Quaker School at Ipswich. At the age of 14 he was apprenticed to Samuel Jesup for eight years. At the expiration of his indentures he moved away. Quaker Samuel Jesup was a grocer, tea dealer, draper and candlemaker, a predecessor of Doubleday's (128).

How would Mr Barton feel if he came back today? His dreams would probably turn into a nightmare. The quiet little country place is much larger and noisier, with people dressed in different fashions, engaged in different trades and professions and much motorised traffic. He would see many more shops with different names over them and hundreds of houses where there were fields and open spaces in his day. The obelisk has been replaced by the Jubilee fountain and the whole town lit up by electricity, replacing his "new-fangled invention" - gas!

The popularity of "Halstead's Heritage" and encouragement of friends and local people spurred me on to compile another pictorial book of the town. It is my wish to take you all back to have a look at Halstead in the past but as most of this book is based on people's memories I therefore apologize for any unintentional mistakes but where possible I have checked the facts. My grateful thanks go to everyone who has helped me, especially Ken Stanhope, Paul Hermon, Dave Osborne and the Halstead & District Local History Society, for the loan of their photograph collections, and I am deeply indebted to the Halstead Gazette for recording our local history for nearly 150 years. My thanks also to all the local people who have given me snippets of information whilst chatting in the street; to Adrian Corder-Birch for painstakingly checking the finished article and writing the foreword, and finally to Brian and Jill Fleming for their invaluable help.

To the following who have helped with information and photographs, please accept my heartfelt thanks.

Mary Aldous, Clacton
Danny Allen
Pam & John Amey
Mike Baalham
Percy Bamberger
Sheila Bayley, Sudbury, Suffolk
David Baylis
Connie Beckwith
Margaret Blogg
Esme Blowers, Colchester
Christine Buscall
Terry Clifton, Hunwicks PLC
Adrian Corder-Birch
Robin Cowling, Ipswich, Suffolk
Susan Cowling, Stowmarket, Suffolk
The late Daisy Cracknell
June Davey
Mary Downey
The late Denis Drury, Gosfield
Peter Drury
Eve Faulkner
Brian & Jill Fleming, Colne Engaine
Barbara Foot, Cornish Hall End
Mollie French
The late Alan Frost, Greenstead Green
Gill Gardiner
Rev. T.G. Gregory-Smith, Barton-On-Sea, Hants
David Guthrie
Gwen Hardy, Liverpool
Paul Hermon, Tendring
Kath Humphries, Basildon
James Hutchins, Greenstead Green
Neil Kibble, Blo Norton, Norfolk
Margaret King, Porthcawl, Wales
Patience Knowles, Spain
Karl Lindekam
Mervyn Lougher-Goodey, Vancouver Is. Canada
The late Father Christopher Maher
John Malseed, Dedham
Doreen Middleton
The late Rose Mortimer
Basil Moss
Margaret Partridge
The late Ivy Randall
Lenna Rayner
Brenda Reason, Framsden, Suffolk
Patricia Rivers
Rev. Eric Robbins, Poole, Dorset
Ian Root, Colchester
Malcolm Root
Richard Root
Clive Runtle, Cromer, Norfolk
Diane Scillitoe
Marion Smith
Mary Smith
Alan Staines, East Horsley, Surrey
Geraldine Stuckey
The Society of Friends
Jim Waters
Alec Watson, Castle Hedingham
Linda Warren, Cherry Hinton, Cambs.
Ronald Whybrew, Stanstead, Suffolk
Mike Yetton-Ward, Stowupland, Suffolk
Essex Police Museum

Contents

1. Halstead Footpath Walkers 1996

A Ramblers Club was formed in 1899 at a meeting in the Reading Room of the Literary Institute (127), to encourage the study of botany, archaeology, geology, local history and other subjects of a more or less scientific character and visits to various local places of interest within easy distance of pedestrians. The group above are the Halstead Footpath Walkers, lined up before the camera at Peterborough on June 2nd 1996 to mark their 200th walk. This club was formed at a public meeting in St James Hall, Ronald Road, in 1987, after the suggestion had been put forward by the Town Council. Marlene Stanhope worked for the Town Council at the time and was made the first chairman. Since its formation many miles have been trodden by their well-attired feet. I'm asking you now to put on your comfortable shoes and take a walk round the town to have a look at the locations where the following photographs were taken. Failing that put your feet up and let your memory wander back.

BLUE BRIDGE

2. Blue Bridge Hill circa 1920

Peace and tranquillity abound in this quiet country scene taken in the 1920s near the foot of Blue Bridge Hill, now the busy A1124, formerly the A604. Peeping out from the foliage on the right are Bluebridge Farmhouse and Blue Bridge House (3). Just look at the smooth, even road surface, very different from that of earlier years. Some main roads then consisted of a tightly packed earth foundation covered with pebbles, which were gradually ground up by passing horse-drawn vehicles. During the 17th century the local surveyor of highways was most unpopular as he had to "turn out the able-bodied men of the parish, to work on the roads for six days a year". Some managed to evade the task when money changed hands. Records show that in 1771 2/4d (12p) was spent on the Street with a massive 7/9d (39p) on Rosemary Lane! The arrival of motorised traffic, in the late 1800s, destroyed the surfaces and sent up clouds of dust in the dry weather and mud when wet. Regular traffic produced deep ruts and potholes making it very dangerous to those on two wheels - thank goodness for Macadamised roads!

3. Painting of Blue Bridge House dated 1787

Before reaching the river from the Colchester direction, you will see Blue Bridge House on the right, looking slightly different from the painting. During the reign of Edward III (1327-1377), it was known as Monchensies, taking its name from the owners, the Monchensi family, lords of Stanstead Hall. In the reign of Edward VI and the following years, the estate was owned by John Coggeshall, who added a considerable part to the old house. The name was then "Collups", probably a corruption of the Coggeshall arms - a cross between 4 escallops (cockleshells). John Morley (4), the Halstead butcher, bought the timber framed house in 1712. Holman says that the house "was pulled down and a beautiful brick structure raised in its room", but Bridges Harvey, who owned the house over a century ago and was a direct descendant of John Morley is quoted as saying that the house was originally built of timber and John Morley enclosed three sides in brick, much of which has been pulled down but the front remains as a lasting memorial to "Carcase" Morley, as he was nicknamed. Over the porch the Arms of the Worshipful Company of Butchers is cut in stone with John Morley's name beneath and the iron gates standing at the entrance to the courtyard are surmounted by his initials. He was always proud of his original calling as a Halstead butcher and annually killed a pig on the Market Hill, for which he received a groat - a silver fourpence piece.

In those far off days, travellers were able to admire a charming sight on the opposite side of the road where the present day woodland was set out with terraces, walks and a pond.

4. John Morley (1655-1732)

John Morley was born at Worthies Place, 11 Chapel Hill (31), on February 8th 1655. The name Worthie comes from a family, originally from Kent, who took possession through marriage, of the Blamsters estate, of which the house was a part. From his humble beginning he became a local butcher with a shop in the High Street, near the entrance to Parsonage Street. He rose to be one of the greatest landjobbers in the country, bringing him great wealth, enabling him to purchase Blue Bridge House (3) in 1712. The following year John was successful in arranging the marriage between Edward Harley, 2nd Earl of Oxford and Lady Henrietta Halles, only daughter of the heiress of the 4th Duke of Newcastle. For this he received a 2½% commission on the dowry amounting to a massive fortune of £10,000. Arms were granted to him in 1722 - the crest was a half-length figure of a butcher, dressed in butcher's blue, holding a pole-axe in his hands and wearing a helmet adorned with red, white and blue plumes. The Latin motto "*Nec errat nec cessat*" means "He never misses and he never stops" - signifying the precision and the energy he put into all his undertakings. He died in 1732 and is buried under the East window in St Andrew's churchyard. The horizontal stone marking the grave bears the Arms of the Butcher's Company of London and is believed to have covered his vault inside the church until alterations were made about 1747. There may have been some doubt whether his remains had been left in the church but the Will of his grandson, signed October 25th 1775, settles the matter, as he requested to be interred with his grandfather's body in the churchyard.

5. Blue Bridge, early 1900s

Water always holds a fascination for children and these youngsters were no exception. They were enjoying a paddle in the River Colne at Blue Bridge during the early years of the 20th century.

At one time the river bed at this point, was covered with boards, making it easier for travellers in horsedrawn carts and carriages, on horseback or on foot, to ford the river rather than risk the bridge. Various structures have crossed here for hundreds of years bearing a variety of names - Ashforde Bridge, after a family surnamed de Ashforde, who owned a nearby farmhouse, Coggeshall Bridge from the previous owners of John Morley's house (3), situated a short distance away and later renamed Blue Bridge. W.J. Evans states, in his book "Old and New Halstead", that the name Blue Bridge is a corruption of Below Bridge, meaning the bridge beyond the town, but William Holman suggests in "Holman's Halstead", that the name came from 'its being painted and coloured in Blew'. John Morley was liable for the bridge's upkeep when he took over the nearby property, and this is when it was first painted a "Varsity colour" and the name changed to Blue Bridge. In 1924, after several accidents, there were complaints about the fence adjoining the bridge being painted "a curious shade of blue, in accordance with the name of the bridge" and under night driving conditions it was invisible in car headlights. A suggestion was made that a single white post at each end of the bridge would help the motorists to see the exact limits within which to drive and would retain the sentimental value attached to the blue painting of the bridge.

6. Brick Barn Farm House and Barn

Until the early 1960s, this well worn path through the buttercups and daisies, was a popular walk to Langley Mill and Colne Engaine from Blue Bridge, but eventually disappeared under the Industrial Estate. The large house on the left is Brick Barn farmhouse, built in the early 17th century. The barn, on the right, was built with very thick red and blue bricks in the early part of the following century and housed stabling for two horses. One night, Duke, one of the farm's horses "escaped" and decided to go for a walk up the brick stairs to the hayloft above. Unfortunately the loft floor wasn't strong enough to hold his weight and when the farmer went to feed the horses the following morning he was startled to find Duke hanging through the ceiling. I was not told how he was brought down to earth again! The barn was carefully demolished in the 1930s and the bricks were transported down the road for building work at Blue Bridge House (3).

Before 1960 most of Halstead's industry was carried out within the town but with the development of the Bluebridge Industrial Estate in this area during the past 40 years, most firms provide employment here along with the smaller Broton Estate in Butler Road.

7. Brook Farm House, Colchester Road, in 1882

People walking in the road didn't have to worry about fast cars, motor cycles and juggernauts when this photo was taken in August 1882, just an occasional horse-drawn coach or cart, or pennyfarthing bicycle. The house has lost much of its front garden due to road widening, to take today's heavy traffic. The wooden farm gate seen on the right was the entrance to a green lane that led to Moon's Farm, through Brick Earth Pasture and Coney Burrows Field. Sadly these fields are now buried beneath Bluebridge Industrial Estate, but descendants of the rabbits still survive. The long low shed further up the hill was part of a brickyard. Clay used in the making of the bricks was dug from the fields behind the farm, hence the name Brick Earth Pasture. William Holman, pastor of the Church of Protestant Dissenters (201) from 1700-1730, writes in his manuscripts about "A capital messuage facing the King's highway on the left hand near the Brick Kiln, leading from Halsted Church to Colchester" which "took its name from a family sirnamed de Ashforde of some note about the reign of King John and Henry III". Brook Farm House fits his description, and the present owner, Mr T. MacDonald, was told a few years ago that the house is definitely mediaeval.

8. Brook Farm, circa 1935

Here we see young Ted Ellenger (right), watching his friend Alec Watson riding his horse in the farmyard of Brook Farm during the 1930s - today this area is occupied by Brook Farm Close. The farm was mainly dairy with a few pigs, chickens and ducks. The Blomfield family ran a brick and tile works at the farm for about 75 years, until the early 1900s, when they moved to Little Maplestead. However, Alfred Blomfield, a tenant farmer, continued to run the dairy with a herd of Friesian cows supplying the milk. Various dairy products were made and sold from the farm and 10 Parsonage Street, until Alfred gave up the tenancy in 1921.

After the outbreak of World War II many young women volunteered to join the Women's Land Army as their services were essential on the land to take the places of farm labourers fighting for their country. Girls from all walks of life, many coming from large cities, joined the organisation and where possible farmers provided board and lodgings. Some coming to Halstead were billeted at Bois Hall (225) and others in a long hut near to where Brick Barn Farm barn (6) stood on the bank opposite Brook Farm. The experience of country life appealed to many of the young ladies who stayed and married local men. After the hostilities ended the hut was converted into a bungalow and Bluebridge Garage erected on land abutting the road.

9. The former "Red Cow" in 1964

As you start to walk down Box Mill Lane, this secluded cottage, the former "Red Cow", is on the right. A great number of years ago, when the Mills (12) were in production, the lane was lined with many little cottages (10), housing large families and accessed over a stream by planks of wood. The menfolk were employed at the mills or on the land, both being very dusty jobs, consequently their thirst was great. Local legend says that the men entered the pub by the rear door, unseen by their wives and neighbours. However, the secret soon leaked out where they had been when many returned home drunk, missed their footing on the planks and ended up in the stream. The "Red Cow" was sold in 1860 and became a private residence. The bars situated on either side of the front door, had flag stone floors and wood panelling round the walls, that remained unaltered for at least a century after the pub was delicensed.

10. Box Mill Row in Box Mill Lane, circa 1900

Nestling on the left of the lane going down towards the river, was this row of 20 little cottages. In 1895 all but four of these dwellings were sold for the grand total of £344. They were all demolished in the 1920s. A row of poplar trees were planted in their place but a hurricane in the early hours of October 16th 1987, brought down eight of them causing damage to six cars and a caravan. The remainder were felled as they suffered root damage. This photo was taken circa 1900 when the river was flooded.

In spite of there being an excess of water in this photo, at one time the lack of it caused problems. With the Box Mill watermill (12) operating on this part of the River Colne, Courtaulds found the amount of water needed to power their mill (29) further downstream, was insufficient to provide enough energy to run the fast expanding silk weaving business. At times the miller at Box Mill held back the water for his own use, resulting in much bickering between the two that eventually ended up in court. They were told to arrange convenient times between themselves to take advantage of the water but Samuel Courtauld decided to resolve the controversy by converting his mill to steam power, enabling the silk industry to depend on a reliable power system and grow into one of the world's great industrial giants.

11. Box Mill Cottages, July 1882

These two cottages still remain at the bottom of Box Mill Lane, but are now just one dwelling. On the extreme right of the photo you can see part of a cottage in Box Mill Row (10) on the other side of the lane. The only other cottage to survive from the 19th century is situated right at the top of the lane - the former "Red Cow" (9). The 1881 Census reveals there were 27 dwellings in the lane, with a total of 119 inhabitants, 34 of these were children. Amongst the adults were:

7 Laundresses	2 Sawyers	2 Gardeners
2 Charwomen	3 Crepe Weavers	4 Domestic Servants
7 Silk Weavers	1 Carpenter	3 Labourers
1 Army Pensioner	3 Millers	1 Draper's Assistant
3 Dressmakers	1 Upholsterer	2 Errand Boys
4 Silk Winders	2 Tailoresses	12 Agricultural Labourers
1 Blacksmith	2 Brickmakers	1 Paper Mill Labourer
1 Newspaper Vendor	1 Maltster	10 Housewives
2 Mechanics	1 Factory Assistant	1 Engine Driver
1 Housekeeper	1 Mother's Help	3 School-mistresses at British School

The fact that all the School-mistresses taught at the British School (Richard de Clare) leads me to believe that the Howe School (116) closed about 1880.

12. Box Mill, late 1800s

As you stand by the river in Box Mill Meadow, near to the footbridge at the lower end of Box Mill Lane today and gaze at the trees and nettles, just imagine what the scene was like for about 200 years, until the early 1920s. This picturesque watermill housed three pairs of French stones for grinding corn into flour to make bread for feeding hungry mouths. In this photo all looks very calm and peaceful, but one morning in July 1888, Walter Wicker, a mill worker made a horrifying discovery. On going to the top floor of the mill, he found the mutilated body of his master, George Ruffle, entangled round the shafting with the machinery still revolving. It is believed that George, after starting the water wheel, was leaning over the stones to put the belt on the main shafting, when he was caught by his coat or beard and dragged in.

The buildings belonging to Box Mill and the Mill House, containing many thousands of good bricks and tiles, with many fine oak beams and timbers, were demolished in 1920/21. What a lovely home it would have made today in such an idyllic situation. Also at this location stood a windmill, built c1775, that met with a watery end during a violent storm (frontispiece). It was in this area that 16 year old Arthur Hart of Ramsey Road, received fatal wounds from bombs dropped by enemy aircraft during World War II, being the only recorded death by Military action in Halstead.

13. Basketmakers in the late 1800s

An area behind Box Mill, where ducks made their home in the osier beds, during the early 1900s, was popularly known as The Duckey, until a prominent townsman explained that the proper name for the marshy land near the river was in fact the Decoy, as ducks were put there in olden days to decoy wild birds, which were afterwards netted. The way into the Decoy was through a gate opposite the Ashlong Grove entrance in Hedingham Road. One gentleman remembered going there as a lad to watch his mother stripping the osiers ready for the basketmaker. Many places by the river were producing osiers for tradesmen like Edward Cranfield (right) and fellow basketmakers.

Basketmaking was quite a popular occupation in the town during the 1800s and early 1900s, with whole families busily weaving the willow. Some names I came across were Robert, Simeon & Elizabeth Archer, David & Joseph Cornell, William & Walter Cooper, Thomas Cadby, Thomas Cudmore, Charles Parsonson (162), David Dixey and Arthur Porter. Arthur had a large shed in the Co-op Yard (214), where Riverside flats now stand. It was here that he soaked the strips of willow in tanks to make them pliable before making baskets of all descriptions, including baby cradles and children's chairs with woven seats. He grew his own willow in osier beds beside the river near Box Mill and at the back of the Golf Links (122). His products were sold in his wife's little shop next to Pendles (165) - now a dental surgery.

14. Box Mill footbridge pre 1908

Crossing over the river at Box Mill, one could admire the countryside and maybe see a train chugging along the Colne Valley, now just a memory. The wooden footbridge caused quite a problem in 1872, resulting in the following letter appearing in the local paper, "Dear Sir, On behalf of Sparrow Trustees I beg to submit that I have done all that is necessary. The holes are filled up, the wharfing is repaired, the railing is made good and the dirty Slough Well coated with gravel. But what of this veritable Box Mill Bridge? - the bridge itself. It is literally a "Bridge of Sighs", bending and broken, rickety and rotten, fatherless and motherless, trampled on by everyone, cared for by no one! On some dark floody night this coming Winter it will be swept away - yes, swept away - And then the ears will ring with the cries of the poor, pitiable foot-passengers (pantalooned & petticoated) carried off headlong by the stream, shrieking, clutching, struggling, gurgling, dying, a horrible kettle of fish - Tell the Board with profound respect I have done my duty. Yours in earnest, Robert Emson." The structure must have been repaired many times following this plea from Robert Emson who lived at Slough House Farm at the time, as a new bridge made entirely of iron and supported by brick pillars was not constructed until August 1908. You may see traces of a hard surfaced footpath leading from the bridge across the meadow to the football ground and wonder why? The answer - in the early 1900s Mrs Courtauld liked to walk from her home, The Howe (118), into town, taking a short cut across the field, so a path was laid enabling her to reach her destination without soiling her fashionable clothes.

15. The Town Bridge, c1914

Imagine this area at the lower end of the High Street, when the only way over to the other side of the river was through a shallow ford - the Town Ford .The river was held back when the Townford Mill was erected in the late 1700s, necessitating a bridge to span the deeper water. In 1828, the narrow bridge was widened as the horsedrawn coaches had great difficulty in negotiating it. The Causeway side was known as the Horse Wash and on the opposite bank was an area where the poorer townsfolk went to collect water for washing etc. In 1846 a new bridge, with a brick parapet and single arch was constructed to replace a dilapidated one. This was subsequently widened twice, a second arch added and some decorative iron railings put in place. The photo shows another replacement structure, 10-12 foot wider on the High Street side, built in 1912, after the Council purchased and demolished a shop occupied by Mr Barker (168). Our present day bridge was erected in 1980 to cope with the modern day traffic. The centre of the bridge was used as the dead centre of Halstead, from where the town boundary was measured in 1854. It had the unique distinction of being a complete circle, with a 1,000 yard radius, but was altered in 1932. The drapery business of William Exinor Dunt, at London House (left), was taken over by John Simmons in 1926, whose family had been associated with the trade in town for over 100 years. After John died in 1962, the family carried on until the business was finally sold to Miss Mildred Head of Sudbury, four years later, when the shop was believed to have been continually in the drapery trade for over 200 years. Demolition took place in the early 1970s.

16. The Bull Hotel, Bridge Street, c1950

The Halstead Gas Company Ltd was formed in 1835 along Rosemary Lane (67). The Gasworks consisted of one gasometer to begin with, a further one being added in the 1880s near to the junction with Chapel Street, when the company was known as the Gaslight & Coke Company. A third gasholder replaced these further along the lane. Before moving up the High Street next door to the White Hart, the Gas Office was a room on the right in the Bull Hotel. Here customers bought a chitty for 6d (2½p), then trundled round to the Gasworks with their old prams and wheelbarrows to collect a bag of coke for the fire. The manager of the Gas Office was Mr F. Arthur Last, who read a paper called The Post. This was delivered to the office by his paperboy, Vic Arnold, who cheekily christened the delivery point "The Last Post".

From the Last Post we go to a first at the Bull. On January 18th 2003, after centuries of serving thirsty travellers and passers-by with refreshers to help them on their way and food to satisfy their hunger, the first marriage ceremony was performed in the hotel's function rooms behind the main building. When Martin Hunt and Marlene Stokes, both of Halstead, tied the knot at 2pm, they made history as the first couple to take advantage of a wedding licence granted to this historic Inn during November 2002.

17. Inside the Bull

The public bar of the Bull Hotel, where these locals are drinking their pints, was the former Gas Office and standing next to the till is Norman Fairman, who hired cars and was chauffeur to George Courtauld. It is said that George left him his immaculate "sit up and beg" model Daimler, when he died and this was garaged at the rear of the Bull and was the envy of many. The photo was taken on August 24th 1943, when the landlord was William Yetton Ward. The "Hotel Review" dated November 1943 speaks of another drinker at this hostelry - "The Bull Hotel goes back to about 1450 and it is on record that Charles Dickens, during one of his many journeys to East Anglia in the mid 1800s, alighted at the Bull, and having adequately refreshed the inner man, as was his wont, strolled up the hill, along Sudbury Road till the coach caught him up". He would no doubt have been pleased that one of his ardent admirers, Morton Mathews, named his house in Sudbury Road, Pickwick House, after one of the characters in "Pickwick Papers", written in 1837. The two seated and one standing near the window are Philip Firmin, Len (Lump) Spurgeon and Charlie Bragg.

18. The Bull corner, Bridge Street, c1900

The Bull Hotel on the left, is one of Halstead's inns that has survived the centuries. Once the stopping place for the London to Bury St Edmunds horse-drawn coaches, we see the Bull today much as it was in those days but the photograph shows the false Georgian front that was removed in 1912. Before the police force was in existence, watchmen were the only persons to ensure the safety of people during the night. There were three watch-boxes - shelters for these men - one opposite Colchester Road, one in Workhouse Lane, now Mill Chase and the other near the Bull. The watchmen would regularly call out the time and the state of the weather. On the right is Argent's drapers shop, demolished in 1909 when the corner was widened. The wall and iron railings in the centre of the photo, bordered the Railway Station forecourt. This was used for many years by the Eastern National Omnibus Company as a bus park. Other companies such as Blackwells, Letches, Jennings and other buses from the surrounding towns and villages had a parking point in The Causeway near the Bull.

19. Bridge Street in 1966

The Crown Café was at one time sandwiched between two public houses, the Railway Hotel and the Bricklayer's Arms. It was conveniently situated for the railway and the buses, allowing drivers and conductors to pop in for a quick coffee, whilst they waited for passengers to board their vehicles in the bus park opposite (20), now Trinity Court. It was also a meeting place for the youngsters of the town and surrounding villages, where they could have a snack and listen to the latest records on the Juke Box. The shop formerly belonged to the Wright family, selling fruit, vegetables and fresh fish and was latterly run by their son-in-law, Ernie Horwood, until he became the landlord of the King's Head (46) in 1936. The fish shop remained open until 10pm when the last train left for Hedingham, thus enabling the homeward bound cinemagoers to buy the fish fresh for the next day as fridges were few and far between. The Railway Hotel (left) was built in 1861, on the foundations of The Angel, once a famous coaching inn. On the other side of the Crown Café was a bakery, formerly the Bricklayers' Arms, a pre 1869 beerhouse and originally three cottages. The adjoining shop ended life as Solly Brewer's Betting shop, and at the end of the row was a cottage next door to a fish and chip shop. All this row was demolished in the early 1970s and replaced by modern shops set further back. Until 1860 Bridge Street was called Chapel Street, extending from the Bull corner to the bottom of Mount Hill.

20. Clover's Mill in 1960

Clover's Mill stood at the junction of Bridge Street and Trinity Street. Built in 1782, this building was once Halstead's House of Correction. Before the Police Force was formed, parish constables patrolled the streets and anyone taken into custody at night was put in a cage in Workhouse Lane, now Mill Chase, then taken to the House of Correction the following morning. In 1841 a decision was made not to repair the building, so all the prisoners were transferred to Chelmsford Gaol, and the premises converted to Halstead's first Police Station for the newly formed Essex Constabulary. Nine years later a new purpose built station was erected in Chapel Street, now Trinity Street (239), and the old one converted to a flour mill. During demolition of the mill in 1969, Eve Faulkner was chatting with two of the workmen, who took her to a location where they had found a complete pack horse bridge of great age. When the river was drained to allow the bank to be made up, the preserved bridge emerged from under the silt in the river bed, near to the present day footbridge to the car park. They also discovered on the mill side bank at the end of the bridge, a small stone lock-up, extremely strong and hard to knock down. The bridge was reburied in the silt where it remains to this day. Halstead's original north-facing prison stood in the vicinity of Trinity Court and was a thatched cottage, rented from the Trustees of Martin's charity. Men and women had separate work and lodging rooms with another provided for the sick. There was no water and their allowance was a pound and a half of bread with a quart of beer a day. The prisoners were engaged in spinning but were allowed no part of what they earned. This prison was burned down in March 1781 - four prisoners perished in the flames, three males and one female - and as a result the building in the photo was erected as soon as possible. Owen Clover, who died in 1904, was associated with the milling trade for nearly 50 years. He took over the former old 'lock-up', which a short time previous had been adapted to a flour mill. The bus park can be seen in the foreground, now part of Trinity Court, with the Railway Hotel on the right.

21. Volunteers behind the Corn Exchange in 1901

When the railway came to Halstead in 1860, it was speculated that there would be a large increase in agricultural trade, therefore a Corn Exchange would be beneficial. It was built by Harcourt Runnacles in 1864, opening the following year, but unfortunately the venture failed, as local farmers had always taken their corn etc to Braintree and could see no advantage in changing. For this reason the Corn Exchange suffered and soon ceased to function. The Colne Valley Railway leased the property as a storage depot until their own sheds were erected. Clover's (20) later hired it for grain storage until 1900. Amongst the following small users were the Halstead Volunteers until the Education Committee accepted a proposal in 1903 that it should become a Technical School serving children from Halstead and local villages as a Handicraft and Domestic subjects centre. It was not until 1907 that the first pupils arrived after complete internal reconstruction plus an entrance porch being added to the Bridge Street end with adjoining public conveniences (since removed). The centre closed in 1968 after Ramsey School (72) was built. The library transferred here from the former Friend's Meeting House (61), officially opening in April 1971 where it remains today. These men, volunteers of "E" Company 2nd Volunteer Battalion, Essex Regiment, were lined up at the rear of the Corn Exchange in 1901, an area which is now the United Reformed Church of Halstead, formerly the Doctor's surgery.

22. The Halstead Allotment Association, c1920

Come along into the old Corn Exchange (21) during the early part of the 1900s to meet some of the hard working gardeners of the town. The Allotment Association was formed during World War I, to stimulate the production of food. During the war years it was very successful and by 1920 the membership had reached 153, but many were not allotment holders. In the background some of the fruits and vegetables of their labours can be seen displayed in large baskets. These men were all committee members of the former "Red Lion" Allotment Association.

Back Row, l to r: Frank Rowland, H.A. Beadle, Frank Davey, Herbert Lock and Herbert Wright.

Centre Row: George Catchpole, George Nash, Dr C. Gordon Roberts, Johnny Moule, Bill Everitt and Harry Rayner.

Front Row: Sam Kensall and Walter Raven.

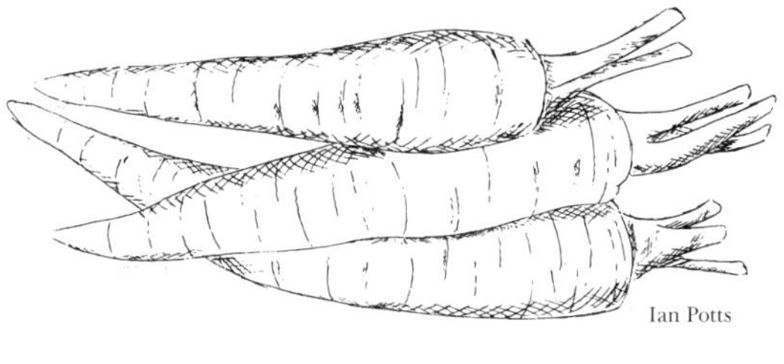
Ian Potts

23. Attention!

After the end of World War II a Victory parade of the armed forces was held through London. A few weeks later these young army cadets waited in the station yard (20) for a coach to take them to the Capital, where they joined other army cadets from all over the United Kingdom for a parade through Hyde Park, in front of Princess Elizabeth, now the Queen, who took the salute. In the background, on the right, is the British Restaurant in Trinity Street, which was forced to close in 1949 due to poor patronage after the price of the main meal increased by a penny to 1/2d (6p). The cadets are: Back row l to r - Dennis Clark, Peter Colyer, Ronald Whybrew, John Wright and Jim Howard. Front row; Peggy Hadley, Molly Kibble, Molly Wright and Pauline Kibble. They were members of "C" Company, Halstead, 11th Essex Regiment, Army Cadet Force and the photographer was another cadet Stuart Pountney.

These cadets would not have liked to have stood in that area before the mid 1800s as drains and open ditches discharged crude sewerage directly into the river along with rain water. At Rosemary Lane the ditches and channels were in an indescribable state, while Bridge Street, a similar collection point for rubbish and foul smelling matter was allowed to exist in the form of an open ditch at the spot which later became the entrance to the Railway Station. The ditch was several feet wide and was crossed by planks. The effluvium arising from the drains was most offensive. About 1837, 100 houses had been erected on Chapel Hill and the Chapel House estate, near the present day Police Station, without any drainage, along with another 90 in Trinity Square (Butler Road). By the end of the 1800s conditions were very different from those of earlier years as the sanitary conditions had improved immensely with a good system of drainage and abundant water supply, proving to be a boon to the health and comfort of the town. Before the waterworks was built it was stated that one poor woman living in the Trinity parish had to make her tea with the same water that she had boiled some cabbage in for her dinner.

BUTLER ROAD formerly TRINITY SQUARE

24. Andrews' shop in the 1930s

Many front rooms of cottages in the back streets were turned over to little shops selling all manner of goods to enable the families to earn a few pence to live on. This one was in Trinity Square, formerly Hildyard's, a watchmaker and jeweller. It later became the home of the Andrews family and was run by Ivy, the wife of Moses. The sign over the window advertises 'Ladies & Gents, Wardrobe Dealer' and inside local people could purchase mainly second-hand clothes amongst other goods. Before moving here the family lived in Head Street where Moses ran a sweet & greengrocery shop. To supplement his income he hawked fruit and vegetables round the houses from his pony and cart. The nature of his business earned him the nickname "Cooking Apple" Andrews. Moses is seen here with his son Hughie during the 1930s. Near their cottage was a cart entry beside Albert Lawrence's bakery leading to Black and White Rows (27). It was related to me that a large room constructed over the gap joining the shop to a cottage was always referred to as Farthing Hall, as the owner had saved all his farthings - a former bronze coin worth a quarter of an old penny - to pay for it.

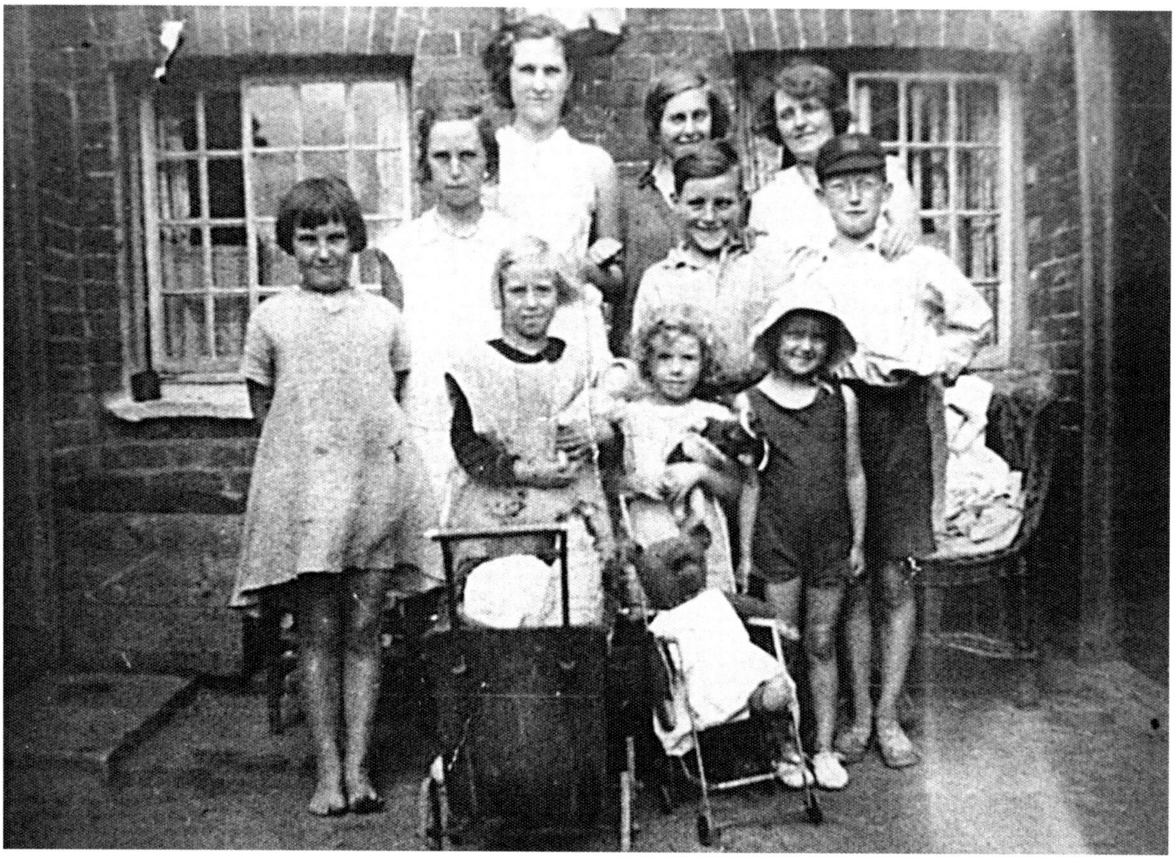

25. Some of the residents of Trinity Square

If you had ventured into the "Square" during the early 1930s you may have seen these children playing, but when a cameraman entered their midst they all stopped to pose along with a few of the mothers. Time was not calculated by a clock or watch but by the trains that trundled up and down the Colne Valley railway line (27).

Back Row l to r: Emily Root, Edna Sudbury and Clara Haynes

Middle Row: Eileen Root, Bernie Andrews and Eric Haynes

Front Row: Joan Clements, Ruby Bacon, Joan Bacon and Joyce Haynes

In 1899, men armed with picks and shovels began creating a road from Trinity Square to Crowbridge at the bottom of Chapel Hill. The area which it dissected belonged to the estate of the Rev Wm. Beridge, landowner, farmer, vicar and owner of a brickfield, off Russells Road behind Halfway House. This road was named Beridge Road for obvious reasons.

26. Part of Trinity Square

Trinity Square, originally called the Found Out, was once very narrow before being widened in 1900, for better access to the new Beridge Road. Here we see the backs of Great Yard cottages that formed part of the Square. The back doors of the dwellings faced each other in pairs and each pair had to share one outside lavatory. The whole area was cleared in 1966 to make way for a Council development of flats, houses and warden assisted flatlets - Colne Valley Close. After the redevelopment had taken place the road was renamed Butler Road, to commemorate the services given to the town by the late Lord R.A. Butler, M.P. for the Saffron Walden constituency, of which Halstead is a part. The 1,000th dwelling built by the Halstead Urban District Council was one of the flatlets in Gladys Malpass House, Colne Valley Close and its first tenant was Mrs L Simmons. When she was presented with her key at a ceremony in April 1968, she was congratulated by Mr Stanley Symonds, a former chairman of the council, who was born in the first house that the council built - Waterworks Cottage in Parsonage Street (193).

27. The Hunt in Trinity Square

Onlookers line Trinity Square, now Butler Road, to watch the local hunt pass by during the 1950s. The signals, on the left, were by the railway line and some of the old cottages are visible behind the telegraph pole on the right. The cottages, of which there were approximately 80 in 1949, were arranged in a large square. Black Row formed one side, White Row, in which 12 dwellings were demolished in 1935, formed another side, where one wall was left and still remains beside Frank Vaizey House. Another side was known as Great Yard, with Little Yard running parallel to it. The fourth part of the square were the cottages lining the road towards the Locomotive. By the 1920s there were only about 50 of them left. Many Council houses were erected during the 1930s, enabling some of the families to be rehoused in Windmill Road, Fenn Road and Harvey Street. By 1963 only 24 of the dwellings were still occupied, but they were all classed as "unfit for human habitation or by reason of their bad arrangement or the narrowness of access, dangerous or injurious to the health of the inhabitants", so the whole area was cleared to make way for the Colne Valley Close development.

Part of the Portway foundry once occupied the site of the Butler Road car park and to commemorate this piece of Halstead's history stands a large model of the world famous Tortoise Stove (216).

28. Inside the Empire, c1915

Thurston's Mobile Picture Palace was set up for a few weeks on the football ground, now the Kings Road playing field, during 1911 and at every performance prizes of meat and coal were given away, even to children - probably much appreciated in those days. Other mobile cinemas visited the town before 1913 when a burly Cockney showman, Tom Keneally, opened up the Electric Kinema in the old St Andrew's Hall (198), boasting of real moving films, not 'flickers'. Two years later the purpose built Empire Cinema opened with a film called "The Light that Failed", and guess what - the lights did fail when the motor generator that ran the carbon arc light failed, resulting in a lot of hissing and booing. Tom, a familiar figure, often seen riding round the town in a donkey cart, later became a manager after the closure of his own cinema. The Empire was heated by two large Tortoise Stoves (216) which were kept red hot in the Winter and were often surrounded by people roasting chestnuts and potatoes. There was always a smell of them cooking and during the films intermittent loud bangs occurred as the nuts burst. After World War I, an economic slump made it hard for people to find money to visit the cinema so in 1923 the two Halstead cinemas were forced to be under the same management, with the Colne Valley (Savoy) continuing to show films and the Empire taking on the role of a Live Theatre, eventually closing because of too much competition with talking films in 1931. After two years it reopened as a cinema and in later years held matinees for children on Saturdays. One manager had a novel idea - he would throw a few ice-cream tubs in different directions during the interval for children to catch, thus getting them to sit down before the second half began. The cinema was kept going by the Faulconbridge brothers until 1971 when lack of support resulted in its closure again, but not its death. A small group of dedicated local people worked hard to raise funds and were rewarded in 1978 to see its doors open once again, for the showing of films and many other forms of entertainment. This is an early photo of the Empire's interior with a grand piano at the front on which a skilled pianist accompanied the silent films with music that portrayed the action and tempo.

THE CAUSEWAY

29. The Causeway, c1900

This much-photographed part of Halstead was once very different. Imagine this scene before the Courtauld family came to town back in the early 1800s. On the right stood tightly packed cottages and the access was very narrow, muddy and strewn with rubbish, much of it finding its way into the river, making the whole area very smelly. The white-boarded Townford Mill, straddling the river, was originally a corn mill and on the opposite side was a tanyard reputed to be Halstead's oldest industry, founded in 1573. The Courtauld houses (right), replaced some of the old dwellings in 1883, being built for mechanics and overseers at the nearby factory. The designer of these was George Sherrin, architect of the Cottage Hospital in Hedingham Road and The Kursall at Southend. On February 25th 1917, the wall by the river suddenly collapsed into the water, carrying the iron railings with it. More than a quarter of a century before, the questionable condition of the wall was under discussion and the builders of the time recommended that it should be rebuilt, but one said it would last another 25 years. He was right - only just! During the latter part of World War I, it was arranged for hot baked potatoes to be provided for people to conserve the bread supply, due to the flour shortage. A portable oven was set up near the Bull from where 900 lbs of spuds were sold in the first three days.

To shed a little light on dark nights a gaslamp was erected on an island at the entrance to the Causeway but in 1923 an out of control lorry demolished it so a decision was taken to remove it altogether.

30. Mill House, adjoining the Townford Mill

Mr Samuel Courtauld (left) and his wife (seated) are seen here posing with three of their staff in the garden at the rear of Mill House at the end of The Causeway. The occasion was to record the departure of the gardener, William Carter (back right), who married Phoebe, one of the housemaids, before emigrating to Australia. The photo was taken about 1908, when Samuel was manager of the Halstead Mill, a position he held for over 20 years. The Courtauld family later moved to Stanstead Hall, where they lived with their daughter Sydney, the first wife of R.A. Butler, M.P., who later became Lord 'RAB' Butler.

31. Prince of Wales' Oak, c1900

At the junction of Mount Hill, Chapel Hill and Trinity Street stood this tree planted in 1863 by Fanny, daughter of Robert E. Greenwood, to commemorate the marriage of the Prince of Wales, later King Edward VII. The tree became dangerous and was felled 100 years later, being replaced by a keep-left sign and a street lamp. The stretch of little cottages 1-13, Chapel Hill are some of the oldest in town. During the late 1800s the first two were occupied by Charles Layzell, a straw plait merchant, and his family. Numbers 7-13 were originally built as one large house in the 12th century, which is thought to have been a monastery connected with the chapel (33) that stood on the other side of the road. As recently as the early 1900s there were still gravestones in the rear garden of No. 13. The house, named Worthies Place, after an ancient family that lived there, was divided into four cottages a few centuries later. Years ago a white veined polished marble plaque over a fireplace in a room, now part of No. 11, bore an inscription in gold lettering, announcing that John Morley (4) was born there in 1655. Adjoining No. 9 is an early Victorian shop that has been a grocers, pawnbrokers, drapery, clothiers and a machinist's shop, where women were employed as dressmakers and milliners and during World War I made army uniforms. It was also used for drying flowers and ended as an antique and second-hand shop. At the rear, now Partner's Electrical, was Scott, a wheelwright and waggoner. The side of the shop still bears the scars of the waggon wheels gouging out the wall as they passed up the yard - Scott's Yard. Along the back of No. 13 there was a long room with a large wooden bench and huge mangle where laundry was washed with the spring water that ran behind the cottages, for people with no washing facilities.

32. Holy Trinity Church, c1900

As the population increased, it was decided to build another church on this side of the River Colne, in 1843/4, on or very near the site of the ancient Merchant's Guild Chapel of the Holy Trinity (33). The architect was George Gilbert Scott, who designed Trinity Church on the Gothic Revival style and whose work can be seen in many English cathedrals and churches. The flint facing covers walls of brick and the doorways, windows, arcades and the spire are all buff grey gault brick. The spire had problems starting on July 20th 1844, when it collapsed 11 days before the church was due to be consecrated. A large crowd and 89 clergy eventually witnessed the event on October 10th of that year, when a full peal of bells was rung with gusto. The weight proved too much for the spire to bear and it developed a twist, resulting in the removal of the bells and the rebuilding of the spire, with buttresses being added to the tower. Mary Gee contributed most of the money, as she did for St James Church, Greenstead Green, erected the following year, also designed by Scott, in which the six bells from Trinity were hung and remain today. With just one tolling bell, the belfry was put to good use at Trinity - a Sunday School room where many children have carved their names and initials all round the walls, over the years. The spire had an unusual 'lodger' for some time when a silver birch tree took root. It was removed and is still growing in the churchyard below. Once again St Andrew's became the parish church for people on both sides of the river, when in 1988 Holy Trinity was "retired" and is now cared for by The Churches Conservation Trust. In the foreground is a building that today is residential but in 1930 was opened as a hairdressers after being converted from a stable and chaise house. After the shop closed down for hairdressing, the premises became an antique shop and has since been converted to a residential unit.

33. "Joe"

If only this stone-faced figure could speak, he would probably be able to solve the mystery of the chapel that vanished, yet gave its name to Chapel Hill. He was found in a large pit under Trinity Vicarage (34) during demolition, to make way for Vicarage Court. The pit contained many lorry loads of stone rubble, including broken pillars, all of which were transported away. "Joe", as he was nicknamed, was rescued by Eve Faulkner and carefully looked after. In 1999 a team of stonemasons arrived at Trinity Church to do some restoration work and examined "Joe". As he was carved from ancient stone they were certain that he was a roof support for inside arched timbers, dating back to 1200 or earlier and not a remnant of Trinity Church spire which collapsed whilst being built in 1844. Was he part of the ancient Merchant's Guild Chapel of the Holy Trinity built on a three-cornered plot of land, now occupied by Trinity Church? Was the chapel smashed down and the rubble buried in the large pit during the Reformation in the 16th century? In his book "Old & New Halstead", W.J. Evans states that the font from the old chapel was taken to 'Simnels', now High Barn Hall and used as a drinking trough after spending some time at a property in Trinity Street.

34. Trinity Vicarage, Chapel Hill

The vicarage was built in the 1840s from plans drawn by William White, an architect of high reputation, described as a conscientious and successful worker in the school of the Gothic Revival. He executed a very large number of works, principally churches, schools, country houses and vicarages all over the country, including St Andrew's (203) and Gt Maplestead vicarages plus the village school. The last vicar to live here was the Rev. Peter Disney, who retired July 31st 1978 and was not replaced. The vicarage was demolished after the church was vested in what is now The Churches Conservation Trust in 1988 and Vicarage Court erected on the site.

In its 144 year history the vicarage was the home of nine vicars and their families, who came to Halstead to serve the spiritual needs of the community.

Rev Charles Burney 1844/5
Rev Duncan Fraser 1845-77
Rev Frederick J. Greenham 1877-89
Rev Charles E.G. May 1889-97
Rev James B. Oldroyd 1897-1904
Rev Albert E. Austin 1904-43
Rev Frederick E. Bayley 1944-58
Rev Charles R. Heard 1959-69
Rev Peter J. Disney 1969-78

For the last 10 years the vicarage was privately owned before demolition.

35. Rose Cottage, Chapel Hill

Rose Cottage, on the right, with an adjoining bakery, stood on what is now a grassy area at the bottom of Windmill Road, until it was pulled down in the late 1960s. Opposite, a row of little cottages bordering the road towards the Bird in Hand were demolished in the same decade. Behind them stood the slaughterhouse of Jack Root, built on the site of a six-roomed residence called Lavender House. In 1930 the Fire Brigade was connected to the phone which proved to be a great advantage and despite the fact that they had to first obtain a lorry to pull the engine, load their gear and travel from Head Street, they reached the fire in 13 minutes. Two bread delivery vans, belonging to Mrs Richardson, and other vehicles were removed from nearby garages on both sides of the lath and plaster house, which was completely destroyed. Did the house take its name from the lavender that was grown locally? Off Chapel Hill, near the Bird in Hand, was Gooseberry Square, said to have consisted of at least eight dwellings - just hovels and to reach the upper floors the families had to climb up outside ladders.

On the opposite side of the road was another of Halstead's yards - Orchard Yard, a row of four little cottages standing in the region of Orchard Avenue, with access between No. 41 and the cottage next door.

36. Chapel Hill in 1955

Danny and Chips Allen were asked to clear an area in Oak Yard, off the High Street in August 1955. On closing a large wooden gate that had stood open for years, a piece of local history was revealed and removed to their scrap yard on Chapel Hill. Danny is seen here seated upon the rare Rudge Quadrant tricycle built in 1884. The original owner was John Pendle, a local postman who lived in Oak Yard in the 1800s. He delivered the mail on this very machine around the Gosfield and Hedingham area. Although the solid tyres were missing and it was somewhat rusty, the overall condition was remarkably good, with almost perfect wooden handle-grips. Besides carrying the mail John enjoyed being a waiter at many dinners and social functions held locally and for more than 26 years was verger at St Andrew's Church. He had six daughters and three sons and died in 1906. His grandson, Herbert, ran a furniture shop at the bottom of the High Street (165) and when the tricycle was found, he recalled riding it himself in 1900. I was interested in trying to find out if it was still in existence, so with Danny's good memory and a phone call I was fortunate to trace its current owner to Dedham - John Malseed, a bike enthusiast who, after researching their histories, restores very old machines to their former glory. The old tricycle is now proudly displayed in Flatford Mill museum for all to see. This photo of Danny was taken in 1955 on Chapel Hill with Crowbridge Farm in the background.

37. Crowbridge in the late 1800s

The Crowbridge area of Chapel Hill has changed considerably since this photo was taken in the late 1800s, from a similar point to that of Photo 36, when the pace of life was much slower. The old cottage on the right, which was quite large, was demolished before Beridge Road was developed in 1900 and Chapel Hill was widened. In 1908, the Halstead Liberal Club opened a Bowling Green at Crowbridge Farm (left), where the soil must have produced luscious grass as the fertility yielded a monster turnip - 27½" in circumference, 9" high and tipped the scales at 11 lb 10 ozs. The oak tree was a favourite place for starlings and one young lad from Trinity Square, out bird's nesting, climbed up to pinch an egg. He inserted his hand and arm into a hole and became firmly stuck. Was the Fire Brigade called? No, Dr Roberts was summoned, climbed up a ladder to release the lad with soap and water, making a clean job of it! Have you ever wondered why the houses on either side of Chapel Hill from the Bird in Hand to Crowbridge are situated on a bank? The reason - before 1862 the hill was very much steeper and higher. It was realised that all the horsedrawn traffic expected to visit the Essex Show at Sloe House (220) that year, would have great difficulty in negotiating the steep incline, so a team of men were given the task of taking off the top of the hill and lowering the road, leaving the cottages on the resulting high bank.

38. The Old Maltings, Chapel Street, in November 1976

This long weather-boarded building was once maltings belonging to Isaac Sewell, a brewer and descendant of a wealthy clothier of a few centuries ago. After many years, the maltings became redundant and served as a granary for Clover's (20), later becoming part of Portway's foundry for pattern storage, early in the 20th century. The building fell into disrepair over the years and mysteriously burned down a few years ago. The brick structure, on the right, was a pottery for some time before this whole area was redeveloped.

Local legend has it that people owing money in the High Street and Head Street shops could sneak down the backway from Mill Chase, through Fleece Yard, across Hedingham Road to continue down to this area via Chapel Street, to avoid being confronted by any shopkeepers. This 'run' became known as "Debtor's Alley".

On the corner of the Chapel Street/Rosemary Lane junction, from 1925, stood a corrugated iron hut used as the Post Office Telephone Linemen's office, later the workplace of a basketmaker. It was supported on brick piles due to frequent flooding from the river.

39. The old Bathing Place, off Chapel Street, c1900

This photo was taken at the Bathing Place on the River Colne, at a wide bend known as Moor's Hole. It was properly organised with corrugated iron bathing huts, two of which can be seen on the left, and three wooden platforms of varying heights for jumping or diving into the water. A caretaker was employed to keep the place in order and to teach young children to swim with the aid of a pole and harness. Both males and females were allowed to indulge in bathing but at different times. Admission was sometimes free but at others a charge of 1d (½p) was made. At the Sport's meetings held annually in August, a charge of a few pence was made for admission to the Bathing Place and enclosure. Spectators could view from the meadow of Mr Evans for 1d or 2d from Mr Nash's on the other side of the river. The sports included - 150 yard race, 100 yard race, diving, high diving, long diving and obstacle racing. There were life saving displays and fishing exhibitions, when young boys were the 'catch' of the day. Water Polo was also played against teams from other towns in the Halstead & District League. When the Bathing Place closed for the season on October 1st 1915, 3,213 bathers had visited the site during the Summer; this is surprising as the Indoor Swimming Pool, in Parsonage Street, was opened the previous year. After a few more years the river bathing place was closed for good. In the background of the photo is Chapel Street and the Rosemary Lane area.

Left to right : the Maltings (70) with oasthouse, the gasholders of the Halstead Gas Company, Portway's foundry and Trinity Church. This view was taken before 1906 as John Bragg (244), the caretaker, died in August of that year and he appears as one of the spectators of this event.

40. The River Colne near Chapel Street, 1963

The Winter of 1962/3 was the coldest in Essex since 1740 and brought misery to thousands with frozen pipes, power cuts and blocked roads. A team of men with two 250 gallon tanks on a lorry, were continuously carting thousands of gallons of water to homes with no mains supply, where residents queued up with their buckets. Plumbers and gasmen were engaged non-stop, repairing fractured water and gas pipes, due to the hard frost. As seen in the photograph, the river froze over making a playground for the energetic near the Paper Mill Bridge (41).

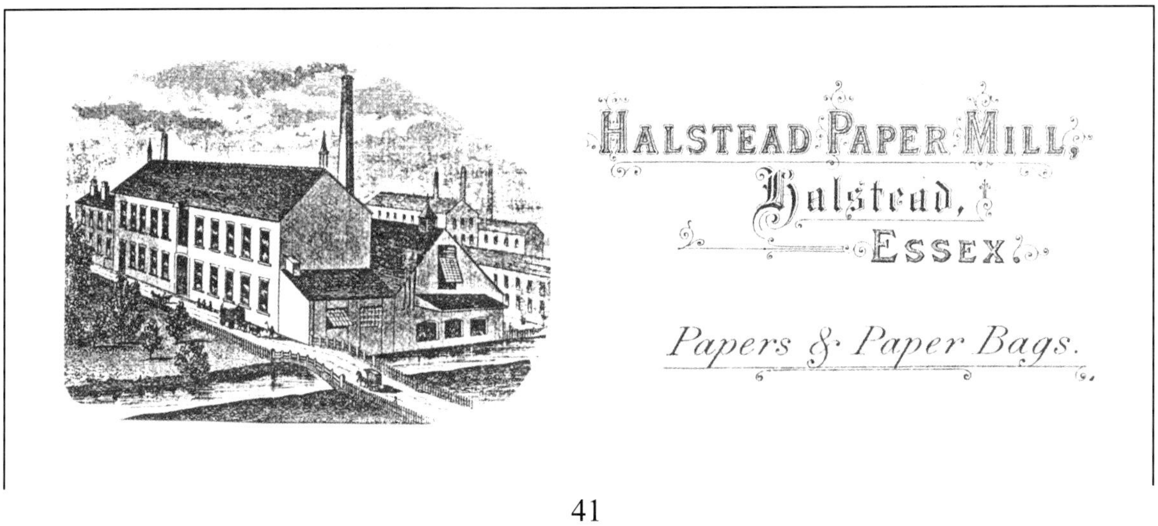

41. Paper Mill Bridge, Chapel Street, 1964

Spanning the River Colne at Chapel Street is Paper Mill Bridge, taking its name from the nearby Paper Mill, which operated in the late 1800s. During 1828 a paper mill began production at Greenstead Green, in a former flourmill at a site to the south of the present day sewerage treatment works off the Burtons Green road. Alfred Potter worked there and when it closed in 1870 the estate and mill were sold. The plant, including an 8-horsepower steam engine was bought by Alfred and removed to Chapel Street, forming the Halstead Paper Mills (on the right). Here he built up a very successful industry, with 30 men and boys turning out about 30 tons of notepaper per week. Alfred was first to introduce the paper trade to the town which he did successfully but came up against a lot of opposition. After 15 years he was forced to move further down the river, where he built the Colne Valley Paper Mill. After a great deal of hassle from the Local Board causing him to make costly alterations, he was running very successfully again when a disastrous flood, in May 1889, completely destroyed everything he had worked for.

I think the Colne Valley Paper Mill was situated near Parsonage Bridge (192), as the flood was recorded in The Essex Standard dated 18th May 1889 - "Considerable damage was done at the Parsonage and the Paper Mill". Also Alfred wrote to the Halstead Gazette in March 1891 about the demise of the paper trade, stating that his neighbour who had recently died had not objected to him. On checking I found that Edward Raven of the Colne Valley Ironworks, Kings Road, was killed on 26th February 1891 and this was just a stone's throw from the river and the Parsonage on the other side of the railway line. The Paper Mill building in Chapel

Street was sold by auction in 1891, when the freehold was purchased by Messrs. Portway & Son. After years of various uses the building was converted into seven dwellings in the 1980s.

In the centre background, at the top of the incline is Bay House, standing at the junction of Chapel and Upper Chapel Street. A mysterious fire gutted the house in 1975 and the present block of flats was erected on the site.

42. Inside the old Paper Mill building c1940

It is hard to believe that families are now living in this building after its conversion in the 1980s (41). The photo shows the inside of the old Paper Mill during the time when it was used by Hunwicks. After the manufacture of paper ceased in the late 1880s, the mill was bought by Messrs Portway & Son for foundry use. Before World War II, Mr W.A. Hunwicks was a general engineer in London and came to Halstead after being bombed out in 1941, hiring the old mill from Portways to set up a business. Mr W.G. Harrison had moved to the town in 1919, where for more than 20 years he was employed by Portways as a works engineer. In 1941 he left the company to join Mr Hunwicks, forming W.A. Hunwicks & Co. Ltd, fabricating engineers, and during the War years the firm turned out many torpedo trolleys for the Admiralty. Mr Hunwicks retired with ill-health in 1944 but the works still traded under his name as it does today at the Harrison Works in Kings Road to where it transferred in 1949.

43. Halstead Tanyard, Chapel Street, c1960

For nearly 400 years Halstead's leather had a reputation of being among the very best in the world and was in great demand for high quality work. It is believed that the tanyard was founded by John Woods, in 1573, on land beside the river opposite The Causeway (29), transferring to Chapel Street in the early 1800s. There were a number of small tanneries in the local district long before this one, some as early as the reign of William the Conqueror. Part of the tanyard was sold to the Eastern National Omnibus Co. (154) in 1938 for a new garage and in 1950 another portion was bought by the Post Office. The year 1962 witnessed the end of a long history of leathermaking in the town when the tanyard, which ceased production two years previous, was finally demolished and levelled to make way for Chapel Street carpark. Many 5-6 foot deep pits were filled in. The animal skins were soaked in lime and water in these, before being transferred to tanning pits filled with oakbark liquor to be 'pickled' for months. In one shed alone there were over 100 pits. I was told that dogs were dipped in these pits to kill fleas!

44. Mr & Mrs H.G. Hughes, 1920

Henry George Hughes, known as Harry, is seen here relaxing with his wife Florence, in their secluded garden behind their home, "Westbourne", 30 Chapel Street. The area, now Bays Drive and 20-30 Chapel Street was once a large garden belonging to Henry Lake Hughes, Harry's father, whose favourite hobby was gardening. He took great delight in his pleasant grounds bordering on the river, where he spent most of his leisure hours. The family lived over the Post Office (150) until moving to 30 Chapel Street, a house that Henry had built about 1900, when more room was needed for extensions to the Post Office. The garden was always open for people to enjoy. Children of the Baptist Church Sunday Schools, run by Harry and Florence, were able to play games, have treats and go boating on the river as were the Young Men' Institute, known as the "Tute" boys, of which Harry was the leader. He also ran a Bunny Club in his garden where young lads bred rabbits to sell in order to raise money to send to missionaries in Africa. He was connected to many organisations in the town, including the Halstead Urban District Council. He started as assistant to Stanley Moger (98) before setting up his own Valuer & Property Agency at No. 29, one of the terraced houses adjoining his home in 1921. Harry had Westbourne Terrace built in 1904 to accommodate the families of Tannery employees who worked opposite (43). The name Westbourne was taken from a Building Society with which Harry was once connected. He took over the Halifax agency in 1946 and retired on December 31st 1956, allowing Geoffrey R. Copsey to come into the business the following day, continuing until his retirement on August 31st 1996. The Halifax then transferred to Messrs Scott Maddison, Estate Agents, next door to the White Hart occupying the former gas office at 17 High Street.

45. The Tree House, Chapel Street

Completely hidden away from passers-by was the Tree House built in an old orchard behind Westbourne, 30 Chapel Street during 1968/9. The Long Span Timber framed structure was commissioned by Dr Larry Collier, a local general practitioner. The natural surroundings were incorporated in the design rather than destroyed to make room for it. A pear tree grew up between the split-levels and apples, on a gnarled tree, were within easy picking distance from the patio roof. Originally intended for a holiday retreat in their spacious garden, the tree house was the brainchild of a friend, architect, Walter Segal. Once built, Dr & Mrs Larry Collier fell in love with it and decided to take up permanent residence themselves, selling their original home, Westbourne, in 1971. The whole structure stood on stilts mounted on concrete slabs, doing away with foundations, and was assembled by one man simply using a spanner and screwdriver. Many trees were uprooted in the garden during the hurricane of October 1987, but the house escaped damage. Entrance to the house was from Upper Chapel Street on the right of Westbourne. In 1997 the large garden and tree house were sold for redevelopment, resulting in its demolition for the building of Bays Drive.

46. The King's Head, Colchester Road, c1940

A public house had stood in this area for 200 years. The original building, situated nearer to the road, was demolished in 1937 and replaced by this larger one. As Colchester Road was then classified, the pub had to be set back 60 feet from the centre of the road to provide a "draw-up" in front. The new King's Head opened in April 1938 with Mr Ernest Horwood as tenant. It was a 'local' in more than one sense of the word - built with local materials by a local builder, Mr J.S. Norton, and local labour. The roof was reed thatched by a Norfolk thatcher, but sadly on February 17th 1962, this thatch was destroyed by fire, after which the roof was tiled as we see it today. The King's Head closed its doors in the early 1980s as a pub, reopening in 1984 as a Sports and Social Club. This venture was short-lived and the building was converted into a private home called King's House. The post supporting the King's Head sign now stands beside the Gosfield Road (242).

One Halstead family, the Humes had the distinction of holding the licence of the original King's Head for a total of 70 years, starting with William in the 1860s followed by Eliza, Walter and ending with Emily in the early 1930s.

47. Courtauld's Bowling Team, c1929

Courtauld's Sports ground, covering about seven acres, was officially opened on June 3rd 1922, a generous gift of Samuel Courtauld to the employees of the Halstead factory. Facilities for many sports were laid out by the groundsman, Mr P. Gould, including a bowling green of six rinks, four tennis courts plus cricket, football and hockey pitches. Before the sports ground was opened bowls was played on the lawn behind the Mill House (30). The club was affiliated to the County in 1921 and celebrated its 75th anniversary in 1996.

The Bowls team of 1929 from left to right:

Back Row : Ernie Horwood, John Shaw, George Curtis, Barney Tuffin, Gerald Brown, John Curtis and Dick Basford.

Middle Row : John Smith, Ted Dean, George Thompson, Louis Widdop, Sam Pye, John Pearce and Charles Goodwin.

Front Row : Bob Potts, Will Knowles, Bert Brewer, Wally May, Charlie Booth and Charlie Clements.

48. Halstead Girls' Grammar School pre World War I

A site, part of Folly Field, Colchester Road, was purchased in 1907 for the erection of a Girls' Grammar School. This was built by a Cambridge firm, whose tender of £698 was £2 less than that of George Sharp and the architect was Walter Cressall, a local man. The opening ceremony performed by Mr E. North Buxton, chairman of the Essex Education Committee, took place on September 28th 1909, when a large number of influential ladies and gentlemen were present, although the immediate surroundings were in a rough state and the building incomplete. At first the school was for girls, including boys to the age of ten. In 1965 the school was enlarged, then 10 years later was closed as a Grammar School to become part of the Ramsey Comprehensive School and renamed Priory Hall. Between the school and the cemetery was a three-acre strip of allotment land called Bell-Rope Field, left as an endowment for the repair of the bells and ropes of St Andrew's Church. In 1962 this field was bought by the council, with the Colne Road half being incorporated into the cemetery and the lower part used for an extension to the playing area and car park for the school.

49. Nether Priors, Colchester Road, c1930

Nether Priors stands on the site of a mansion house called Pryors, named after an ancient family that once owned it. Way back in 1483 it belonged to Henry, Earl of Essex. Standing at the rear of Nether Priors is Lt-Colonel Charles Withers Ravenshaw, who resided here until his death in 1935, aged 83 years. He joined the Army in 1872, serving in various capacities in India until his retirement in 1906. He came to Halstead six years later and was held in high esteem by the local people. During World War I he was a Special Constable and a keen supporter of the Boy Scout movement, for some time acting as District Commissioner. A previous owner of Nether Priors, G.W. Harris, was senior partner at Messrs. Harris, Morton & Harris, solicitors of Halstead, of which his son Frank was also a partner.

Halstead Camera Club was formed at Nether Priors in June 1893 by a large number of people to whom amateur photography had become a "favourite amusement". Katherine, only daughter of G.W. Harris, became president and Stanley Moger (98) undertook the duties of secretary and treasurer.

During World War II the house was used as Air Precautions Headquarters, then in 1946 it was compulsorily purchased and used as a hostel for non-sick aged persons. Three years later saw the conversion to a home for 20 elderly people - all the men being ex-service. There was another change in 1976 when the home became Nether Priors Hostel as it is today.

50. The Executive Committee of Halstead Gala, 1894

This group of Halstead's leading citizens posing before the camera in 1894 are:

Back Row : William C. Sheen, the local registrar; Dr. C. Gordon Roberts, Medical Officer and physician; William Turnell, landlord of the George Hotel; Edgar J. Potter, School Attendance Officer; W. Drane; William Errington, Master of the Workhouse; J.W. French, Walter Yerbury, headmaster of the British School; Thomas S. Bates, cycle-maker.

Front Row : Obadiah Kemp; Edward R. Smith, saddler and mail carrier; Harry Portway, foundry owner; Frank Harris, solicitor and President of the Committee; Rev. J.B. Andrewes, Chairman and curate of St Andrew's; Alfred W. Kibble, general manager of Portways; and Frank M. Wallis, veterinary surgeon.

These men certainly worked hard to entertain the local population. It is recorded that the Gala of August 1894 was held at Nether Priors (49), the home of President, Frank Harris. The programme for the day included - stage attractions, musical comedians, singers, dancers, conjuror, illusionist, Negro minstrels, pianist, the Fancier's Society with poultry, pigeons, cage birds, cats and rabbits, a Dog Show, Flower & Vegetable Show, the Town Band, needlework exhibition, athletic sports, cycle racing, blindfold race, gymkhana, steam circus, fancy fair, shooting gallery, coconut shies and Earls Colne Brass Band. Trains were arranged to bring people from Haverhill, the Colnes, Chappel, and Sudbury. This certainly paid off as approximately 7,000 attended, more than the population of the town.

51. Armoury Cottage, 87 Colchester Road

At an auction on January 11th 1859, Harcourt Runnacles, a local builder, bought a piece of land situated in Colchester Road, part of Mill Field, bounded on the north by the cemetery and adjoining a sand and gravel pit. Two cottages were built on part of the land, referred to as the Old Sandpit circa 1890, with an armoury attached to No. 87. This was the single storey, on the left, where rifles were stored and was rented to the War Office as a yearly tenant. Sergt-Instructor Marchant lived in the house and was responsible for recruiting "desirable" young men for the 2nd Volunteer Battalion Essex Regiment. The two cottages went up for sale by auction in 1914, when Harry Honey Goldsmith was a sitting tenant in the armoury cottage. In that year he was ex Colour-Sergt Instructor to the local branch of the Territorial Force and was the recipient of a gold watch chain and locket to mark the appreciation of his services. He joined the Essex Regiment in 1884 and had 30 years service. In 1899 he took up duties at Halstead as Instructor to the old Volunteer Force, in charge of the Armoury and acted as trainer to the Territorials when they were brought into existence. I am indebted to Prunella Bibby, a local artist, for the impression of the cottage as it was before alterations.

52. St Francis of Assisi, about 1930

In 1897 Cardinal Herbert Vaughan stayed at the George Hotel for three days, in order to make a pastoral visit to the Catholics of the town, to meet the Rev. T.G. Gibbons, vicar of St Andrew's, and to give three lectures on the Catholic Church in the Town Hall (127) next door. It was decided that Mass would be celebrated in Halstead once a month. After meeting in a private house until March 1898, a Catholic chapel was established at the old ropewalk (214) in Rosemary Lane. This venture was shortlived, due either to the lack of support or funds, ceasing to exist about 1901, necessitating the Catholics to travel to Bocking Convent, many of them walking. In 1926, Madame Edith Arendrup, granddaughter of George Courtauld (1761-1823), and daughter of John Minton Courtauld (1807-1877), came to Halstead to visit the poor and at the same time inspect a plot of land, for the purpose of building a church. Edith was previously a Unitarian becoming a Catholic before her marriage to a Danish Army Officer. Tragically her husband was killed in battle two years later and following the death of her son at the age of 20 years, she became a nun. In 1927 she went to live at the Franciscan Convent, Bocking, formerly Bridge House, the Courtauld family home, where she was born 84 years earlier. The result of her generosity was the little timbered church in Colchester Road, now the Parish Hall, which was dedicated to St Francis of Assisi on September 29th 1928. Over the years the congregation outgrew the building and it is said that in the early 1950s Dr Richard Minton Courtauld, of Perces, Greenstead Green, was unable to enter the church because of overcrowding and later sent a cheque to cover the cost of building the present one situated beside the 1928 construction. The new church was also dedicated to St Francis and was opened on October 12th 1955.

53. The Rev. Fr. G.N. Gresley

Father George Nigel Gresley is seen here feeding the birds in his garden at 85 Colchester Road. His brother was Herbert Nigel Gresley, the famous designer of locomotives and chief mechanical engineer with the London & North Eastern Railways, who was knighted for his achievements and known as Sir Nigel Gresley. Father Gresley was born in 1865, a son of a Derbyshire vicar and was ordained as a vicar himself in 1888, but for unknown reasons was unhappy in his living and left the Church of England in 1917, later converting to Roman Catholicism. After spending some time studying in Rome he was ordained as a priest in May 1928 and on returning to England was appointed the first parish priest at St Francis of Assissi (52) at Halstead on September 28th 1928. Two years later he moved into 85 Colchester Road with its spacious garden, next door to the Armoury Cottage (51). One day, whilst crossing the road from the church to his home, he was hit by a lorry, sustaining a broken leg which forced him to retire. He moved to Clacton where he sadly died on August 22nd 1938 aged 73 years and was buried in the cemetery behind his former home in Colchester Road. Coincidentally, some years later, Father John Roche was knocked down whilst crossing the road at the same place, also sustaining a broken leg.

54. Part of the Cemetery on October 16th 1987

A five-acre strip of land, part of Mill Field, between Colchester Road and Colne Road was purchased in 1855 by the Burial Board, to provide a cemetery for the town. This opened the following year, with a second part consecrated in 1877. More adjoining land was secured for future burials in 1919 when the Burial Committee had the foresight to buy a piece of land for future use, that was sold by auction. This area was set out with ornamental trees and evergreens to give an appearance that would match the original cemetery and was consecrated in May 1933. A long strip adjacent to the old unconsecrated ground was reserved for Non-conformists and a far corner backing on to the old sandpit (51) was set aside for the burials of Roman Catholics. By 1999 all the grave spaces were accounted for necessitating interments to be started in the former Bell-Rope Field (48). The little flintstone building was erected many years ago as a "Mourner's Protection", for use during inclement weather, and during the hurricane of October 16th 1987 it escaped damage from the uprooted fir tree, and over 40 surrounding mature trees that were toppled or badly damaged.

55. The Town Bowling Green

These gentlemen are playing bowls at the Town Bowling Green situated between 42 Colchester Road and the Grace Baptist Church (56). Before May 1919, the Chantry Club played on ground at the rear of 18-20 High Street, then the office of Morton & Son, and former home of Samuel Fiske (135), until this new green, formerly a tennis court, was obtained. Five years later, a 75-foot long ex-Army hut was purchased and after several alterations were made, became the pavilion. Unfortunately the Club suffered a big loss over the purchase of the ground and pavilion, resulting in its winding up in 1930. The land was sold and two detached houses built on the site. The pavilion was taken over by Gerald Brazier for his wireworks business until the late 1960s. It has since been demolished and a bungalow erected on the site.

Another bowling club was situated on land beside Rosemary Lane near the football ground and was run by Portways. The club was formed in 1920 when bowls and quoits were played in Kings Road before moving to Rosemary Lane five years later. In 1932 a brand new pavilion was erected for the use of members, then 44 years later it was dismantled and removed to Castle Hedingham Tennis Club where it remains today. The only bowls club left in Halstead is Courtaulds (47).

56. Colchester Road, c1910

If you had stood at the bottom of Pretoria Road in the early 1900s and looked in the Colchester direction this is what you would have seen. Young lime trees, planted in 1902 and hedges lined the road, only a few houses and an absence of traffic. Behind the hedge between the chapel and No. 42 was the Town Bowling Green (55). The Particular Baptist Church was founded originally in a cottage, moving two years later in 1839 to its first permanent home in a privately owned chapel that was eventually purchased in 1866. The chapel stood on land that later became part of the Greenwood School (177) and the first minister was printer, Samuel Keevan. In 1909 the Greenwood School committee wished to extend their buildings already surrounding the chapel on three sides. The trustees of the chapel were approached with an offer to buy their building and provide a new one on a suitable site - this was accepted. The new chapel was opened for worship in January 1910 in Colchester Road, being the first building to be erected on the farmland. The Providence Baptist, as it was named, now Grace, used to perform mass baptisms in the River Colne at Box Mill. These events were recorded to have drawn many townsfolk to the scene out of curiosity. Looking at this quiet road brought back memories to me of the times when Diana Rayner and I, (we lived next door to each other at 64 & 66 Colchester Road) used to play tennis in the road. One evening whilst playing under the street lamp the ball ran into the gutter and as I retrieved it a man's voice boomed out "Oi, you can't bend down there, you haven't got a rear light on". It was the local bobby on his bike and luckily he could see the funny side of it. On another occasion a lorry ran over our ball which stuck in between its double wheels and disappeared along the road.

57. St Andrew's Schools

A school bearing the name of St Andrew's is believed to have been in existence since 1813, this being a Sunday School, where reading and writing were taught. By 1828 a daily school was being run for girls only, boys being included during the following decade and later provision was made for infants. A National Society's Church School Enquiry records that in 1846, 70 girls, 85 boys and 115 infants were being educated somewhere in the High Street. At that time Head Street was called High Street and the school was the large building overlooking Head Street (92). Lucy Greenwood wished to expand her Industrial School (177) and it was then in 1876 that John T. Adams, of Firwoods, then called Stone's Grange, on Tidings Hill, generously gave a gift to erect a school in Colchester Road. The young children were educated here until 1974, when the school moved yet again, this time to a new site in Mathew's Close. The building in the foreground was for the Infants, with the older pupils being taught in the classrooms at the rear. White brick air-raid shelters can be seen on the left. The whole area was cleared and redeveloped as Saxon Close opposite the Woodman in the 1990s. A feature was left here near Colchester Road - a World War II Spigot Mortar Base which once served as a support to lob bombs along the road if the event of an invasion occurred. It is situated just to the left of the photo and fortunately was never brought into action.

58. Colchester Road in the 1950s

After Edward Smith Coldwell designed the new "Woodman" for Messrs Adams, the brewery's own building and repairing staff decided to erect the Inn themselves. Work commenced in the Spring of 1931, taking 16 months to complete. The foreman bricklayer was C. Rayner, P. Arnold, the chief carpenter and T. Cook, the senior painter - all had been with the firm for a long time. Many of their regular men were kept busy along with a temporary workforce, who were taken on for long periods, helping to relieve the unemployment of the time. The first customer to be served after the official opening on July 18th 1932, was Ernest Horwood, who later became the landlord of the newly built King's Head (46). In 1914 Mr Coldwell the architect, went into partnership with John Sewell Courtauld, M.C., M.P. (1880-1942), trading as Coldwell and Courtauld. He also designed the Homes of Rest in Hedingham Road (112) and the present Ashford Lodge in Sudbury Road, built on the site of a previous mansion destroyed by fire in November 1922. Three Grammar School (48) girls can be seen on their way home in the early 1950s, wearing their Summer uniforms. There were still many lime trees lining the road in spite of complaints during World War I about horses eating the foliage whilst standing in the roadway. The cottage, just in view on the right, was one of a pair that stood at the entrance to the market (59). Years ago there were many old cottages in this area.

59. Halstead Market, c1900

For hundreds of years Halstead's Cattle Market was held on the Market Hill and by the 1880s was still taking place on Tuesday afternoons. The sales were then conducted by Bentall & Robinson, their office being at 23 High Street. For health and safety reasons these were stopped, much to the disgust of local tradesmen, who relied on the stock sales bringing people into town. At this time Stanley Moger (98) came to Halstead and joined the business. The following year, 1893, he became sole proprietor and soon arranged for the stock market to be held on ground at the rear of the Three Crowns (138), resulting in the biggest sale they had held. This venue carried on until Stanley opened his new sale yard in December 1898 on a piece of land, once occupied by many old cottages, acquired from William Cook (103), lying between Colchester Road and Parsonage Street. Everyone was happy as business was carried on more privately and stock was able to be sent the previous day and kept overnight. A cart entrance led from Colchester Road between the present day Chinese takeaway and an old cottage, with footpath access from Parsonage Street. The live-stock market continued until World War II, when it became a furniture, tools and bric-a-brac sale yard, ending up as a car park in the mid 1900s. Stanley Moger is seen here conducting a sale with his assistant Harry Hughes (44). The houses in the background are in Mallows Field.

60. The Labour Party Hall, 1977

How many people travelling along Colchester Road, realise that this building started life in 1902 as a church of the Plymouth Brethren? In 1888, after a visit from Mr W. Johnson, an evangelist from London who preached on the Market Hill, a Mission was started in the town. Services were originally held in a room at the rear of the Bull, before land was purchased next to St Andrew's Schools (57) late in 1901. The hall was erected by Halstead builders, Messrs Alfred Suckling, large enough to hold 200 people. A caretaker's cottage was attached at the rear and called Mission House. After the church ceased to be used as a place of worship, it was let to many small users including a School of Dancing run by Mr & Mrs Greatorex in the 1950s, followed by the Saffron Walden Constituency Labour Party as their headquarters and now goes under the name of Blomfield House, an insurance office.

A local Board of Guardians was formed as a result of the Reform Act 1834 and held their first meeting at the George Inn on November 9th 1835. In 1923 with money raised from the sale of the workhouse (111) the Union office was erected in Colchester Road (left). On March 7th 1930 the Board's last meeting took place as from April 1st the administration came under the control of Essex County Council. Since then the building has served as the Clinic and is now a nursery school.

61. The old Quaker Meeting House in 1977

This Meeting House was built by the Hornor family of the Howe in 1850/1 to accommodate the growing numbers of Quakers in the town as they outgrew the building in Factory Lane East (73). The Quakers took a keen interest in education and were instigators in the founding of the Greenwood School (177). During World War I the Meeting House became a local Y.M.C.A. depot called the "Soldier's Welcome", where local people and the soldiers themselves entertained the troops. Soon after the war the Quakers were prominent in the founding of the Adult School for men, held on Sunday afternoons in the Co-operative Rooms, Trinity Street, but after 30 years this came to an end. In the mid 1930s the Halstead Library moved into the main hall of the Meeting House where it remained until transferring to the old Technical School (21). During this time the Society of Friends suffered from lack of support after the passing of the oldest and most influential members, resulting in the last meeting being held in 1970, with the sale of the building in 1975. The burial ground situated at the rear was flattened to make a car park in the late 1970s after the premises became Brenda Toys. The headstones of many of the local gentry, the Doubledays, Hornors and the Greenwoods, including Lucy (176), were replaced along the boundary wall.

62. Part of Colchester Road from the air

This aerial view taken in 1949 shows part of Colchester Road that has seen some changes over the years. The large building near the centre with the flat roof was the old Quaker Meeting House (61), with Arundel House, now the Chinese takeaway, beside the road. Frances Abbott and her sister ran a private school here for about 20 girls in the mid 1800s, assisted by their aunt Caroline Wood, who died in July 1917 in her 101st year. Her life spanned the reigns of six monarchs - George III, George IV, William IV, Queen Victoria, Edward VII and George V - and many inventions that we take for granted - railways, air travel, motorised vehicles, gas and electric. On the left between Arundel House and an old cottage, now demolished, was the entrance to the Market (59) at the rear. The Woodman is visible at the left front and where the pub car park is today was the business of Mossford's, monumental masons, where previously had stood more old cottages including Sunny Yard. The large L-shaped house to the right of the Meeting House caused a great deal of interest in January 2002 when a valuable sewing box was shown on the BBC's Antique Roadshow from Ottawa, Canada, that originated from Moonshiney Hall, this very house, 6 Colchester Road, the home of Mrs Inman. Edwin, Jennet and Zoe, children of a Liverpool doctor, author of many medical books, came to Halstead with their mother in 1882 when Edwin acquired a solicitor's practice at the house. The sisters remained there after the deaths of Edwin at an early age and later their mother, and the sewing box belonged to them. Jennet was very interested in the Esperanto language, running a well attended class to teach others. She died in 1941 at the age of 93, an invalid for eight years after a fall. Zoe was interested in handicrafts and art, producing many paintings of people and landscapes. She was often seen carrying out her skills in her tree shrouded garden accompanied by her faithful Old English Sheepdog. After her death in 1953 at the age of 95, the house was demolished and the site incorporated into Evans Electroselenium.

63. St Andrew's Lodge, Colchester Road, c1954

St Andrew's Lodge occupied a site at the Colchester Road end of the churchyard which is now a garden area. For many years this large house was a family home of various local builders, with a yard at the rear. Runnacles, Woodman and Sharp were the latter owners but the earliest I could find was Abraham Rayner way back in the 1840s, who was grandfather to Harcourt Runnacles (1832-1893). Evans Electroselenium Ltd purchased the area and started production of photo electric instruments in 1952 and the Lodge was converted into offices that had the misfortune of catching fire when staff had to be rescued by ladder from the upper floor. Originally the firm was founded by Arthur Evans in a barn at Potter Street, Harlow with just two workers. The builder's yard was redeveloped in 1962 and the new factory was officially opened by Mr R.A. Butler, then Home Secretary, on May 5th. The firm latterly was Bayer Diagnostics. The Lodge was demolished in 1959. Up until the mid 1800s Colchester Road was known at St Andrew's Street.

64. Red House, Colchester Road in the late 1800s

Prior to 1773, the area on which Red House and the Queen's Hall now stand, was divided into several ownerships and each had a number of cottages. In that year all the property passed to James Sparrow of Gosfield, who sold it the same year to Edward Barron, of Halstead Lodge, now Ashford Lodge in Sudbury Road, a saymaker. In turn it passed to Peter Edwards in 1786, a gentleman from Bethnal Green. It appears that Edward Barron erected Red House before the sale to Mr Edwards as the deeds start with "all that newly erected messuage ...". Edward Barron was described as a farmer and wool merchant, who appeared to carry on his trade at the property, for included in the sale was "a building for depositing and warehousing wool, an accompting shed and a weighing house, abutting upon Scrambler's Lane". This was the lane leading from Colchester Road to Chipping Hill, beside Red House. The whole property sold for £635 and there must have been at one time no less than 25 cottages on the site as the deed describes further - "One messuage, 25 tofts (a small piece of land on which a dwelling house formerly stood), one warehouse, one coach house, 3 stables, 2 curtilages (courtyards), 2 gardeners and 2 ways". The property remained in the Edwards family until the grandson of the latter owner sold it in 1868 to Harcourt Runnacles, a builder, for £950. Harcourt built a wall across the back of Red House and used the rear part as a builder's yard and workshop, leasing the house to various gentlemen for 12 years. The Adams family of the brewery (23) then bought the property in 1893, which was leased to a number of tenants until 1936. The name Red House did not appear until 1893 when Edgar and Percy, sons of Thomas Adams bought the house. The rear portion of the property was sold separately by Mr Runnacles, which Adams purchased too, five years later. They pulled down the dividing wall and converted the land into a garden. The Council acquired Red House from Francis Adams in 1936, adapting it to meet the requirements for offices. These were opened by R.A. Butler in July 1936 and served as the Halstead Urban District Council Offices until transferring to Trinity Street (237) in 1965. Red House was also the Register Office and can boast of at least one famous bridegroom - Thomas Hoar Stevens married here in 1963, with his moustache shaved off, a false tooth filling a well-known gap, plus horn-rimmed spectacles, Terry Thomas, the filmstar successfully had a quiet wedding as he went unrecognised. The Register Office closed in Halstead during November 1972 upon the retirement of James Hines, Superintendent Registrar and was then included in the Braintree Registration District.

Doctors Wright and Watney used the annexe at the rear of Red House as a surgery, which is known as The Surgery to this day. In 1969 an elderly lady, who had not seen a doctor for over 50 years, entered Red House and asked Adrian Corder-Birch if she could see the Doctor. She was either a very healthy lady or was suffering from amnesia. Red House is now the office of Birkett Long, solicitors, previously Smith, Morton and Long.

64a Sir Ronald Long (1902-1987)

Sir Ronald Long held the unique distinction of having been a qualified solicitor for over 60 years and for 45 years was senior partner of Smith, Morton & Long. He was President of the Suffolk & North Essex Law Society in 1951-52 and became Chairman of the Criminal Injuries Compensation Board of which he was founder. He reached the peak of his profession when he became President of the Law Society and was knighted in 1964 in recognition of his services. He had a long association with local government, was Deputy Superintendent Registrar for many years and Commanding Officer of 1163 Squadron, A.T.C. 1941-45. Sir Ronald was still a practising solicitor and consultant when he died in 1987.

65. St Andrew's Church before restoration

Most of the present day church dates from about 1320 but it is believed that a place of worship has been here since the early 1200s. Various parts were added during the following centuries including the North and South porches. Many years ago very few people had timepieces so relied on the church bells to call them to worship. The ancient tower was much shorter and the villagers of Greenstead Green, then known as Stanstead Manor or Leet, could not hear the bells so the belfry was raised with a spire set on woodwork supported by four wooden pedestals topped with an octagonal lantern. All this structure was covered with lead and surmounted with a weathervane. Unfortunately in 1701 this "architectural glory" was struck by lightning, setting fire to the top and burnt downwards melting the lead. This endangered the church, so the wooden supports were hacked down causing the spire to fall into the churchyard with tremendous force. Dr Samuel Fiske, an apothecary, who "dispensed physic" at 18 High Street, paid for a new spire in 1717 which also met with the same fate 60 years later. Dr Fiske was a great benefactor to the town having already paved the market place, given a treble bell to the church and with riches he had acquired did much good. In October 1803, eight local men had the task of erecting a 52 ft pole on top of the church on which to fly a scarlet flag to warn inhabitants of an expected invasion by Napoleon Bonaparte. A third spire was erected but by 1848 the whole church was in a dilapidated state. The roof was propped up and the wooden spire in which the belfry was situated plus galleries all round the church at this time were in urgent need of repair. During one violent storm the service came to an abrupt end and the congregation evacuated for fear of the whole building collapsing. This event was witnessed by Alice Porter when a young girl in the 1840s. At this time, when the church was in desperate need of renovation, a rate was levied on the whole town to help pay for it and there were many legal battles. The following years saw much restoration and alterations creating the church we see today. During renovations in the mid 1800s the bells remained in the churchyard and were still used to serve their purpose. By 1851 £5,000 had been raised and in 1862 a new organ was installed with all the pageantry of Victorian ceremonies.

66. View over Halstead in the 1920s

Halstead is not very often viewed from this position, so whilst we are up here have a good look round. This photo was taken from the top of the church tower in the 1920s before the Council houses were built that now cover much of the farmland on the far side of the town. The two large chimneys were attached to Courtauld's powerhouses. The one on the right was the first to be built in 1904 (76) in Factory Terrace, being made redundant in 1922 when a new powerhouse replaced it in Factory Lane West (80), now Maycast-Nokes Precision Engineering Ltd.

67. A view from the church tower, c1900

Turning slightly to the right of the previous view, one can see part of the town photographed at the turn of the 20th century. The complex of sheds in the centre were in the tanyard (43) and behind the row of trees lining the river is Rosemary Lane with Portway's foundry and the Gasworks. To the right of the large gasholder stands the Maltings (38), complete with oasthouse. The little houses in the background were in Trinity Square, with White Row at the top forming one side of the square. The two gasholders were replaced by a third further along Rosemary Lane towards the football ground, in 1908. This held double the capacity, stood 60 feet high and was the first one in the country in which rivets were clenched by means of compressed air - all 36,208 of them!

After he was demobbed from the Army in 1920, Arthur Nice joined the National Omnibus Company, reaching the rank of inspector but decided in 1949 to do clock and watch repairs. At the same time he took over the responsibility of maintaining the Town Clock situated in the church tower and for over 25 years climbed the 43 steps leading up the spiral staircase to the clock chamber four times a week, to wind up separate mechanisms for the time, chimes and strike, with a key resembling an old car's starting handle. The clock commemorated the Golden Jubilee of Queen Victoria in 1887 and the following year the weight of the chimes fell through the belfry floor into the church below.

68. A bird's eye view from St Andrew's Church

Going round to the other side of the tower and looking towards the old water tower (70), this is the scene you would have viewed about 1910. There were many ancient dwellings, now demolished, tucked away in small yards behind the buildings on Head Street. Chipping Hill and the Queen's Hall area was where the local market was held a few centuries ago. Chipping comes from the Saxon word 'ceap', meaning price and applied to a market. The market was moved there when coming in the possession of Abel St. Martin in 1250. It has been suggested that the original market was held at the foot of the High Street, near the old Guild Hall (166). In the middle of the 1500s, the market was moved again, this time to the Market Hill, at the top of the High Street, where it is still held today. On September 4th 1890, the Halstead Gazette recorded - "One good thing the Local Board have recently achieved - they have taken away a reproach from among the inhabitants of a certain locality in the town, which was hitherto rejoiced in the appellation of 'Sooty Square'. The origin of this somewhat unpleasant name is due to the fact that chimney sweeps have from time immemorial showed an unwarrantable predilection for residing at this place, which now rejoices in the name of Chipping Court". One of the sweeps, William Elymas Newton, who died in 1936 at the age of 91 years had lived there all his life. He started work at nine years old helping his father, also a sweep, and carried on the business after his father's death, retiring at the age of 80. The Queen's Hall is visible in the photo, next door to Chipping House. It has been in existence for a considerable time before being reconstructed, rebuilt and equipped by Stanley Moger in 1924.

69. The church bells, 1904

During the mid 1800s St Andrew's Church was renovated but by 1890 the interior walls were suffering from acute dampness, due to the churchyard being much higher than the floor level inside. A decision was made to have a better drainage system, so Harcourt Runnacles was called upon to remove the earth all round the church, down to floor level and pave a drain to carry away the surface water, as we see today.

In 1903 the six church bells had become very worn where the clappers struck so it was decided to have new fittings installed and the bells quarter turned. A proposal was made at the same time to collect sufficient funds to pay for the work and add a chiming apparatus to enable hymn tunes to be played. The bells were taken down on January 30th 1904 and sent to Messrs Warner's foundry in London to be retuned. This photo was taken about six weeks later when the bells and two new trebles were ready to be rehung. By August 1904, all the money required to pay the bill had been raised from Garden Parties, with 2/6d (12½p) to spare. Outside the North porch, behind the large bell in the centre, is William W. Cooper - 40 years a bellringer, 50 years the Parish Clerk and 63 years a chorister. As Parish Clerk he saw the church organ moved from under the tower to the chancel, the East window altered several times, a heating system installed and the introduction of surplices and cassocks. He witnessed 790 marriages, 2,661 baptisms, 1,723 burials and the installation of the Town clock in the church tower.

70. The Water Towers off Colne Road

A map, dated 1625, shows an area of enclosed land, by Head Street, called 'Painters', with a house and pond. This was Paynter's Pond, which originally overflowed and formed a swift and prolific stream running down Head Street and the High Street, eventually entering the river by the Town Bridge. This stream was channelled underground during the 19th century by means of a barrel arch. The water supply before the 1860s was obtained from wells, springs, the river and small streams. The river water was described as being "hard and of a disagreeable odour", yet in spite of this was still used in the brewing trade. Scarcely any of the working classes had a full supply and many had to go great distances to collect it, sometimes from wells polluted by sewer leakage. In 1862 it was suggested to the Board of Health that there was a great need for a water supply in the town, as many ill people could not even wash their clothes for want of water. Two sites were suggested for the waterworks - Mount Hill and Paynter's Pond. The latter was chosen and the site bought for £50. The following year, John Rolfe, whilst employed in sinking an artesian well in connection with the waterworks met with a nasty accident. The machinery at the mouth of the well gave way and he fell 140 feet to the bottom. Fortunately water in the well was deep enough to cushion his fall. The foreman descended on a rope and held him at the surface of the water until both were hauled up, Rolfe suffering from shock and bruising. Incidentally the soil dug up from the sinking of the well was used to fill in Paynter's Pond. During 1864/5 the town was thoroughly drained and the waterworks established, supplying the town with abundant pure water from the 300 foot deep well. The original water tower built in the 1860s, is on the left, with the larger 1890s one on the right. Both are now redundant but still stand as a permanent reminder of how an abundant supply of water was harnessed in the 19th century to make Halstead a healthier place.

71. Sketch of Halstead from the Sloe Hill area, c1830

East Mill, a very impressive smock mill built in 1800 on an end or head of land by Dead Lane, now Colne Road, seen in this sketch to the left of St Andrew's Church, was described as the finest in the county. In 1862 on Christmas Eve, it caught fire and burned so furiously and rapidly that it was considered useless to call the Volunteer Fire Brigade as there was no sufficient water supply in the vicinity. As the mill stood on high ground the spectacular fire was seen for miles around. It was described that "No fireworks ever exceeded this scene for beauty and magnificence". When the top fell in carrying the sails with it, one immense body of flame rose, lighting the whole town. In spite of it being midnight the church clock was as visible as at midday. How the fire started was a mystery but it was suspected that tramps had taken up residence in the outhouse and had caused it by smoking. The following day, Christmas Day, hundreds of sightseers made their way to view the remains of a one time magnificent building. Before the fire there were two windmills on the eastside of East Mill - a post mill stood approximately 50 yards from Colne Road, on the site of East Mill Bungalow, with the imposing smock mill a further 35 yards south.

72. The Ramsey School, Colne Road

This site, on which the school stands, was previously a field. A map dated 1831 names it Walnut Orchard Pasture, but in later years it became known as Coggeshall Pieces. The meadow was where cows grazed amongst the buttercups and daisies, Halstead Town played football, children played and pupils from St Andrew's School were led in crocodile file for rounders, being careful to avoid the cowpats! An unusual event took place here on Good Friday 1915, when a 'huge throng' of local people plus 300 soldiers, stationed in the town, gathered to witness an award ceremony. Halsteadian Sgt. Percy Pudney, of the Essex Regiment was the recipient of the Distinguished Conduct Medal from Col. Adams, for extreme gallantry on the battlefields of Flanders. There were proposals in 1947 to build a Secondary School at Mitchell Avenue or on the site of Bois Hall. These fell by the wayside and the school was eventually erected on this field and officially opened by Rt. Hon. Lord R.A. Butler in September 1967. With the amalgamation of Earls Colne and Halstead Grammar Schools with Halstead County Secondary, the Ramsey School was formed in 1975, taking its name from Dame Mary Ramsey (145), founder of the Halstead Grammar School for Boys in 1594. Colne Road was once called "Dead Lane" as this was the route used to take dead bodies, victims of the plague, to be buried somewhere over the fields at the top of the Colne Engaine hill near Paddy Crow, probably near where the old Pest House stood (223).

73. The old Quaker Meeting House, 1977

There is evidence of Quakers meeting in a cottage somewhere in Clipt Hedges, now Factory Lane East, and still referred to by some locals as The Clippers. After gathering there for some time, it was decided to erect a Meeting House, consisting of two large rooms and a large gallery, on this site in 1670, following a visit to the town from George Fox, one of the founders of the Society of Friends (Quakers) three years previous. Meetings were held here until increased numbers forced a move to larger premises in Colchester Road (61) in 1851. The building was then purchased by Courtaulds and the Nursery for children of the married women employed in the factory was moved here from the Factory Home opened for the benefit of unmarried work-women of good character, at the south entrance of the town. Due to bronchitis being rife, causing mothers to keep their children at home, the Nursery closed in September 1853. As far back as 1857 this little building behind the wall was occupied by the Unitarians, a Free Christian Church founded by Samuel Courtauld, under the ministry of the Rev. John Robertson. An Evening School for Courtauld's "out town" girls was also held here until 1880 and during World War I and the following depression it served as a soup kitchen. Many local organisations continued to hold functions in the hall where Doris King was well known for running a kindergarten before demolition took place in 1985 to make way for a car park.

74. Factory Lane East

This photo shows Factory Lane East in the days when Courtaulds, the textile giant was in production, giving the false impression of a quiet little lane. When the weavers were at work the noise was deafening, with the click-clack of hundreds of looms. The tall building in the centre was the original engine-house later converted to the canteen. A gable end now marks the spot and is a feature of Solar car park. Affectionately known as The Clippers by locals, the lane was originally called Clipt Hedges, due to being flanked by tall clipped hedges. The two blocks of terraced houses on the left, were built by Courtaulds in 1872/3 for the workers, with an extra storey where out-town workers could lodge. In 1861 a quarter of the town's workforce was drawn from outside Halstead, mostly single women, lodging during the week and going home at weekends. In 1801 the population was 3,380 but by 1861 it had risen to 7,500. This increase was mainly attributed to the establishment of the Silk Factory by Samuel Courtauld. When silk weaving was first introduced locally there were various masters supplying work to the weavers but Samuel was the main one, with the distribution centre in the building that became the engine house. The weavers collected work from there and took it home to weave on their handlooms. Between 300-400 people were employed in this way, weaving silks and satins for dress materials, velvet, umbrella and parasol silks. This accounts for all the weavers' cottages that were once spread around the town. This method of weaving continued until the introduction of power looms, cheaper and faster, making the handloom practically extinct by 1890. The velvet industry gave employment to 800 weavers but was succeeded and ousted by the silk industry. One such weaver of velvet was George Collins who lived all his life in Weavers Row and was one of the last of the old Halstead weavers when he died in 1925 aged 83 years. Both his parents were in the same occupation until velvet weaving began to decline locally. George then became a handloom weaver in the Courtauld's Lodge, formerly situated in Factory Terrace. He carried on working as a departmental clerk, retiring at the age of 80 years.

MARY MERRYWEATHER

Mary Merryweather was born into a large Quaker family about 1820, at Longham, Dorset. She grew up among a large circle of educated upper class ladies with strong social consciences, eager to improve the conditions of the poor. These included Madame Louis Belloc, mother of Hilaire Belloc, writer and politician, Barbara Leigh Smith, who ran Ragged Schools for the poor London children and granddaughter of Wm. Smith, a colleague of Wm. Wilberforce in the anti-slavery campaign and Elizabeth Fry of Prison Reform fame. From a conversation with a friend in Bloomsbury in 1847, she heard about a fete given at High Garrett to the Courtauld management the previous year, by the employees of the Essex Mills. They had met to entertain their employers and to present them with a medal designed and produced for the occasion along with several silk banners with "mottoes and devices expressive of the good feeling existing between them and their masters". After the event Courtaulds wished to do more for the workers by way of educating them and looked for a lady to undertake the job. From these chance remarks Mary applied and was soon appointed to start an evening school for the mill girls at Halstead's Silk Mill. She helped also to organise a nursery for their children, started a library, visited the sick in their homes and became Head of the Factory Home for mill girls at 65 Chapel Street, now called Trinity Street. One 94 year old lady, in 1925 recalled her memories of the mid 1800s when Mary visited employees as Courtauld's representative. She remembered the starting of the night school at the Girls' British Schoolroom (now Richard de Clare Infants School) where Mary, assisted by Milly Green, taught young girls to read and write, proving to be a boon and blessing to many, changing their habits and attitudes. To begin with about 120 "noisy girls, with no womanly reserve or modesty", pushing, jesting and swearing at each other, turned up to receive free education, and due to Mary's efforts they were soon being commended by Mrs Courtauld for their quiet, respectable behaviour. Mary records the difficulties that occurred at first - the road from the High Street to the schoolroom was through a narrow path called "Clipt Hedges" where at the time there were no lamps, the room itself was without gas and sad disasters happened with the oil lamps with which they had to manage until the gas was laid on the following year. She writes how uncomfortable it all was at first down the dark, winding, narrow way necessitating her to carry her own little lantern when she was accompanied by the more timid girls - gas street lighting did not arrive until 1854. Mary describes how noisy groups of rough factory girls used to yell and scream in the dark constantly alarming her, but all this stopped when the ringleader was suspended from work for a while. In the Winter of 1850, the Rev. William Clements, the Baptist minister, was engaged by the firm to educate the men and boys at an evening school in the Boys' British Schoolroom. Courtauld workers were taught free and others, mostly shop assistants, had to pay one penny a week. After 14 years Mary left to train as a nurse in preparation for an appointment she was offered as Superintendent of the Liverpool Training School for Nurses. At this time Mary wrote a book entitled "Experiences of Factory Life" - a record of her work in Halstead. She died on May 5th 1880.

75. The beginnings of the factory chimney

As you stroll along Factory Lane East today, stop and look at the gap between the two blocks of terraced houses. It is hard to believe that a large chimney once stood there. This photo was taken in 1904 when the builders had just begun to erect it to a height of 120 feet, to take away the smoke from Courtauld's boiler house situated on the other side of the lane. After 18 years the powerhouse was made redundant when a new one was built in Factory Lane West (80). The original boilerhouse was converted into a canteen but its memory still lingers on with the gable end forming a feature beside the Solar car park.

76. The Factory chimney, 1904

The previous photo showed the early stages of the building of the factory chimney but here we see the finished article from behind the houses. The two men fitting the cap, consisting of 12 cast iron sections made at Portways, can be seen standing on the top. They had the unnerving task of bolting the sections together and securing them in place. The chimney dominated the skyline until February 1969, when the cap was removed - the sections were unbolted and dropped down inside the chimney. After 65 years the cap was in excellent condition so the metal was bought by Allen's scrapyard and returned to Portways where it was smelted down to be used again. The brickwork was removed some months later by the same method due to the close proximity of the houses - definitely not a Fred Dibnah job!

77. Inside one of the weaving sheds

A peep inside one of the weaving sheds at Courtaulds reveals some of the hundreds of looms that took over from the cottage industry of handloom weaving. During the years of World War II weavers produced 16 million yards of nylon fabric for man-carrying parachutes and thousands more for flares etc. Originally parachute fabric was woven with silk but was later replaced by nylon. Mr W.H. Nankivell was made an O.B.E. in the New Year's Honours List of 1946, receiving it on behalf of Courtauld employees, for their co-operation towards the War Effort. The following year, due to labour shortages, men were employed to weave, previously an occupation for the ladies. Just before the closure of the mill in 1982, caused by cheap foreign imports, there were 632 water jet looms, with one weaver attending to 60 or more looms. All that is left in this old photo are the iron roof supports that have been incorporated on the outside of the Solar supermarket.

The following photo shows the vastness of the factory. One part that survived the demolition was the Spooling, the building with many windows, situated by the river where two mottoes were painted on the girders in the roof - "WEAVE TRUTH WITH TRUST" and "HONOUR TO WHOM HONOUR IS DUE".

78. Courtauld's factory in the 1970s

The Courtauld story started in Halstead way back in 1825 when Samuel Courtauld assisted in the conversion of the Townford Mill (29), from a cornmill, acquiring the same for the weaving of silk one year later. Weaving was done on the top floor until 1832, when a purpose built power loom factory was erected next to the old mill. Extensions were made during the following years as the firm gained worldwide fame for black mourning crape. By 1873 the workforce numbered 1,337, most of them females. In 1886 further extensions were erected, known locally as "California" and "Crystal Palace", because of the glass roofed structure, with another weaving shed being added nine years later to house the Hattersley looms. There were now 1,000 looms and the mill became one of the largest of its kind in the country. Yet another great weaving shed was erected in 1923 in which automatic looms were installed. This view, from the top of the Silo (213), reveals the large area covered by the factory, now occupied by Solar and Millbridge. Architects designed a new complex to blend in with two of the existing buildings - the Redrawing, now Solar's warehouse by the river and the Gauze Room, previously the Spooling, The Surgery, Gatehouse and the blacksmith's shop still survive and Weaver's Court takes its name from the past. Millbridge flats are built on the site where once the weaving was done.

79. Halstead Council School, c1918

Plans were drawn up by Messrs Goodey and Cressall in 1909 to build a new elementary school to cater for 400 pupils. The official opening took place on October 25th 1910. At that time juniors and seniors were taught, but in 1932 it became a senior school only with the juniors being transferred to either St Andrew's (57) or Holy Trinity Schools. A large increase in numbers necessitated a new senior school being built in Colne Road (72) in 1967. The Council School then became a junior establishment and was renamed the Richard de Clare County School in July 1981.

The photo was taken circa 1918 of some of the pupils and two teachers - Morton Mathews and Daisy Taylor, standing at the rear. Daisy was nicknamed "Pills" as her father was a chemist.

Back Row : left to right - Velda Beckwith, Elsie Smoothy, Vera Harvey, Kitty Rayner, Gladys Chaplin, Ada Kemp, Muriel Springett and Ethel Hume.

Centre Row : Hilda Parker, Elsie Heavingham, Mabel Rowson, Lily Norfolk, Winnie Deal, Kathy Owers, Daisy Straight, Hilda Kensall and Phyllis Wookey.

Front Row : Lil Potter, Dolly Harrington, Edna Wicker, Betty Steed, Olive Diss, May Heavingham and Winnie Warren.

80. Factory Lane West from the Parsonage Street Crossing Gates

This view of Halstead, taken in the 1950s, has changed over the years. The silo (213), in the centre, has been demolished along with both chimneys and the railway is now just a memory. In 1896 the Co-op purchased the land on the riverside of the road, known as Cocksedges Meadow, frequently used by travelling fairs, where a series of buildings were erected for the running of the Society. During 1949 a new bread bakery was put into production having been converted from redundant stables, as all the horses had been replaced by motorised transport. Four years later the slaughterhouse adjoining the bakery was converted into a bread slicing and wrapping department. Many years ago Factory Lane West (right) was often referred to as Cocksedges Lane and later locals nicknamed it The Cut or Coal Road, due to the coal yards situated beside the railway.

On December 8th 1899, after the 7:10 pm passenger train had passed, a 16 truck goods train, waiting in a siding, set off before the points were altered to switch it on to the main line. As it reached a speed of 30 - 40 mph the driver H. Bartholomew, Fireman J. Roope and Guard H. Turp had no idea anything was wrong until it reached the buffers, tearing up everything in its path and demolishing the signal - box before toppling over. The crossing gateman, Harry Tibble, had seen the train on the wrong line and waved a red warning lamp to no avail. Harry also shouted to two ladies waiting at the crossing, to get out of the way which they did - quickly!

81. H. Cocksedge & Son, woodturner, Factory Lane West

H. Cocksedge & Son had been a family run business for over 100 years before its closure in August 1963. Henry commenced work as a woodturner with a treadle lathe in an old cottage in Head Street before moving nearby to the rear of the old Black Horse, now No. 55 (90). He continued to carry on the business of a general turner and maker of croquet sets until transferring to Rosemary Lane in 1884, to part of the old Colne Valley Ironworks. For some time he supplied power to the Tortoise Works by burning wood chippings. Six years later he had to vacate his part of the premises and moved to Factory Lane West. His son, Fred, left school at the age of 11 years to join his father, going into partnership with him in 1896. He eventually carried on the firm, being succeeded by his nephew Alec and finally great-nephew Walter after World War II. In 1875, the firm commenced turning polo balls as the result of a casual visit to the turnery mill by the servant of an Indian Army Officer home on leave. The ones made in India were part made of bamboo root, but the man knew that willow ones were better. Soon Cocksedges were supplying most of the polo balls used in this country as well as exporting to India. Travelling showmen were regular customers for coconut shy balls and the 'duds' that served as coconuts. Many locals will remember the spinning tops that kept the workers busy every Saturday morning supplying a queue of children with three pennyworth of firewood and a half-penny top. Road traffic increase put paid to the spinning top lark. When sensing the danger to kiddies whipping the tops along the roads, Mr Cocksedge burnt his entire stock. The two men in front of the sliding door are Fred (left) and his father Henry Cocksedge. Maycast-Nokes now occupies the site.

82. William Warner in his workshop

In 1848 there were at least 22 boot and shoe makers and repairers in the town, but one by one those "old fashioned" craftsmen of a bygone age dwindled away. By the 1970s there was just one left, managing to make shoe repairing a full time job - William Warner. He came to Halstead in 1948 and went on a course to learn a trade enabling him to set up his own business in a small brick building on Railway property with access from Kings Road. Until 1925 it had been used by the Post Office Telegraph & Telephone linemen, as an office and store. When the Electric Motor Development factory was built in 1971, William had to transfer his business to a small plot near to the silo (213) in Factory Lane West but was uprooted yet again when the new Solar store and the former Courtaulds site was developed in 1985/6. His workshop measuring 24 ft by 10 ft was in the way when the road needed to be widened for access, so a crane was used to lift it further back on a piece of land where the Dr Elizabeth Courtauld Surgery is today.

83. Road traffic accident in 1903

This must rate as the worst accident involving the churchyard wall, occurring on April 30th 1903. Joseph Smith and a workmate, Henry Deal, had delivered a load of bricks to Pretoria Road from the Rev. B. Beridge's brickyard, near Gosfield, entering from Colchester Road and leaving by the "Rose & Crown" (92), where a short break was taken. Difficulty was experienced in restarting the traction engine and when finally on the move it was thrown out of gear, resulting in the driver having no means of controlling the speed. He stuck to his post, but his mate leapt off when the machine gathered momentum as it rolled down Head Street. Not wanting to cause a disaster in the High Street, Joseph tried to steer the 'monster' round into Colchester Road but ended up embedded in the churchyard wall with tremendous force, knocking down several yards of brickwork. Luckily he was not seriously hurt. Messrs Raven & Son were called upon to remove the engine the following day, when a large crowd assembled to watch the operation. Whilst this was in progress Mr & Mrs E.T. Adams, from the brewery (236), were passing by in a brougham when their horse was frightened by the noise and "plunged about nearly upsetting the carriage and causing a general scamper of onlookers". Things always seem to come in threes and the third occurred when the engine was in Raven's yard. The Rev. Beridge went to inspect the damage with Edward Raven, who promptly fainted and fell backwards hitting his head on the engine, causing nasty gashes. The engine was subsequently bought by Walter Raven, repaired and had a long life as a fairground engine. A suggestion was made at the time that the corner should be widened. Whether this was done is not clear but previously during the mid 1860s the road was altered by taking down and rebuilding the 'unsightly' wall considerably lower to show off the church to its greatest advantage and many graves were disturbed. Six decades later during gas repairs it was discovered that the wall had at one time extended out much further. Now nearly a century later the corner has recently been altered again to try and stop continual damage caused by large lorries.

84. Colchester Road and Head Street junction, c1900

As you reach the end of Colchester Road today you are faced with a T-junction, as were travellers in 1900 when this photo was taken. Before the 13th century, at this spot there were crossroads, the road to Cambridge continuing straight across. In 1250, when a Market Charter was granted to the Lord of the Manor by King Henry III, there was little room to hold a market in the cramped confines of the town, which had grown up round the crossroads. Consequently the town was extended down the hill towards the river creating the Market Hill. It was important to collect tolls from passing travellers, so the Hedingham road was diverted from its original route near the 'Dog' to the present one, thus bringing people into the market where tolls were collected. When the photo was taken Baker & Son, drapers and milliners, were trading in both the shops directly ahead. Later a passageway was made between them and they were run separately. The shop on the left has been the Wool Shop for decades but the one on the right has had a variety of uses from a hobby shop to the Clinic where children dreaded the white-coated man who ordered them to "open wide"! A public house called the Bugle Horn once stood on the site of Bakers and the house adjoining had a balcony reached by the aid of outside stairs.

85. Head Street during the late 1800s

It had always been a mystery to me that before 1860 there were dozens of shops, businesses and schools in the High Street, yet it was obvious that most of the buildings were large houses. Luckily I came across an article in an old Halstead Gazette that solved the puzzle. Originally, the name High Street applied to the whole length of the road from Paynter's Pond (Colne Road), down to the Townford Bridge (15). The name Head Street only came into existence after the formation of the Halstead Local Board of Health and many of the aforementioned shops etc were in this part of the previously named High Street. This view of Head Street was taken over a hundred years ago, yet looks very much as it does today - minus the traffic. The land each side of the roadway was formerly in the Manor of Abells but was gradually encroached upon by houses being built along the frontage of others set further back, making the street very narrow.

Isaac Brazier's wireworks and shop (right) stood on the corner of Colchester Road, where he and his three sons made anything with wire - sieves, fireguards, garden arches, birdcages and traps. He started his business in 1870 at the Causeway moving to Head Street in 1882, where he worked for 20 years. His grandson, Gerald, carried on the trade in the old Bowling Green Pavilion in Colchester Road (55) until he retired in the 1960s.

86. Nos. 10 & 12 Head Street in 1965

Displayed in the gable end of 12 Head Street is S.K. 1891, not all that old you may think. Samuel Knight's premises before that year consisted of a large billiard room occupied by a private club. At the rear, stables and a cartlodge with a spacious granary above, overlooked Runnacles builder's yard, now the Queen's Hall. One Saturday evening at 9.30, in February 1891 the town shops were full of customers and the footpaths crowded with walkers, when a cry of 'Fire' sent everyone scurrying in the direction of Head Street. A serious fire was discovered in the stables which soon spread to adjoining buildings. Gentlemen were in the billiard room, including Mr Brady and Harry Portway, both members of the Volunteer Fire Brigade and two others passing by rushed home to don their uniforms. The flames soon enveloped the whole of the premises and gradually spread to three of the four adjoining cottages that stood between the club and Braziers (85). Other volunteers soon arrived and a messenger was sent to the Surveyor to bring the fire hose. Unfortunately the hydrant could not be found as workmen had covered it whilst repairing the road. Acting on people's memories the hydrant was eventually dug up but only a trickle of water could be obtained due to low pressure and the bad condition of the leather hose. Whilst all the water was being turned off down in the valley to increase the pressure, another hydrant was found in Colchester Road, but the hose would not reach the fire. Twenty men with buckets were stationed in the builder's yard to stop the fire spreading in that direction. With all the frantic onlookers getting in the way, lost hydrants, insufficient and faulty hoses and a poor water supply, two hours passed after the initial outbreak was discovered before the water began to flow. This is the reason for the rebuilding date of 1891 being on a building in a very old part of town. After the rebuilding, Samuel Tyler, auctioneer and estate agent opened his office and was joined by young Bertie Owers, who became his partner, later taking over the business. Until 1908 No. 10 was the property of Geo. Sharp, a local builder. It then became the Local Tax Office where Bertie carried out the duties of Tax Collector for Halstead and eight adjoining parishes, until the work was centralised by the Inland Revenue in 1936. Also in 1912, Bertie became the manager of the Unemployment Office in the same building, a position he held until his death in 1951. Some of the jobseekers had a lucky escape in 1921 when a disused well gave way just inside the Labour Exchange. The well extended under the pavement outside for about a foot and ran several feet under the office floor. It was 40 feet deep and 4½ feet wide with brick sides and was very old - no doubt used as a water supply for the cottages said to have stood on the site. The well was just covered up with earth concealing oakbeams, which eventually gave way. The water would have been beneficial 30 years previous to put out the fire! In 1965 when the photograph was taken, No. 12 was occupied by Balls and Balls, Auctioneers and Estate Agents.

87. Head Street, c1900

A traffic free view of Head Street taken over a hundred years ago when there were many little shops in the town, some just a room in a cottage. One such business was that of Robert Ridgewell, on the right. Originating from Sible Hedingham, he went to London where he was apprenticed to the boot making trade. Whilst there he met his future wife, also from the same village. They returned in 1896, married and set up the business at No. 23, now 47 Head Street, where Robert worked for 43 years. His son Herbert followed in his footsteps lower down the street at No. 5 after serving an apprenticeship with Mr Percy Walls (156) in the High Street. Further down Head Street, on the right stands Finsbury House. During the early 1900s Samuel Tyler was the occupier, running a nursery on ground at the rear, specialising in pot plants, palms and ferns, with over 10,000 plants to choose from. The house for a brief time in 1918 served as a Red Cross Hospital, then became the Head Office of Newman & Clark's corn merchants for many years, before moving to Kings Road where the office also went under the name of Finsbury House.

88. Head Street during the 1970s

A stroll up Head Street years ago was much safer than it is today, yet there was much more going on. Before 1900 there were at least 38 shops, businesses, plus a few public houses. The double-fronted white house in the centre, now No. 28, was once a pub called The Lamb. It was sold in 1863 with the adjoining premises, said to have been part of the pub, where John Risby was a Marine Store dealer from 1850 until the late 1860s. The Lamb is said to have lost its licence due to illegal cockfighting, once a popular 'sport'. The single storey Lyncombe Hall was erected in the early 1900s, on the site formerly part of the pub, by Stanley Moger who lived at No. 32. The hall was built as a saleroom and an asset to the town, to be hired for meetings and special occasions. During World War II the Gordon Highlanders were billeted there. It was one time the headquarters of the local Liberal Club, also a meeting hall for the Jehovah's Witnesses before transferring to the old Drill Hall (207) in Pretoria Road. The narrow entrance between the house and the hall was a short cut to Manfield via a passageway nicknamed Nine Corners, for obvious reasons.

89. The Chase, c1923

I am indebted to the Lougher-Goodey family of Vancouver Island for making the history of The Chase available to me. It was written by Wilfred Lougher-Goodey from information gathered by his parents during their 40 years residence there. His father Alfred Gladstone Goodey, as many will remember, had a dental practice at The Chase from 1908-1947. An inspection by a member of the Royal Commission on Ancient Monuments in 1927 revealed that the two storied house was built about 1580 and the adjoining cottages of the same date were combined to make one house during the 18th century and in later years, Finsbury Place, a row of weavers' cottage was built nearby. When Alfred Goodey moved into The Chase in 1908 it was obvious that no attempt had been made to modernise the house before. The floors were covered with layer upon layer of cheap linoleum, the walls canvassed and papered or very poorly plastered and anything that protruded was just painted over with layers of inferior paint. The Chase was in desperate need of repair and lacking the ordinary everyday comforts and conveniences to a very serious extent. After removing all the layers of linoleum a very broad plank wood floor was revealed - "good old English oak, as good as the day it was laid". A large bedroom where there was an unpleasant smell was tackled and after removing several layers of paper, paint and canvas (the cause of the smell), the effort was rewarded when oak panelling from floor to ceiling, painted a dirty brown colour came to light. During the residency of Alfred and his family a tremendous amount of expensive restoration work was carried out by local craftsmen and the family, preventing the lovely 16th century house from destruction. The Chase has been a very 'busy' place during its history and has been alive with people. Originally the house was owned by a wealthy wool merchant and was still in the possession of another family with wool connections, the Sparrows, in 1740 when trade was declining, eventually ceasing altogether. In the early years of the 19th century the house became a private boarding school for girls run by Mrs Mary Smoothy and her daughters, and at the same time a Chandler's shop run by Charles Smoothy occupied the east end of the house. He was a Corn, Seed and Hop merchant and a maltster. Evidence of this came to light during the Goodey'

residence when oats kept appearing on the shelves in the cellar below and in the crevasses of the stone slabbed floor. About 1830, someone related that a crude ladder had been used as a staircase leading to an upper room over the shop. Evidence of this was found during restoration. Dr Charles Boreham had a medical practice at the house and being a bird lover had an aviary halfway up the drive. Lucy Greenwood (176), whilst living in what became the superintendent's residence ran a Quaker School at The Chase, training girls for domestic work who had served their time at the Greenwood School and were unable to get employment. Next came Lucy and Emily Worden with their Ladies School and after their retirement two more sisters, Elsie and Edith Hilder, carried on the school from 1900. After the schools The Chase became a dental practice and remained so for many decades and is now a private home.

90. Cottages in Head Street in 1964

Whilst Ken Ketley was converting an old shop and cottage, second and third from the right, during the early 1960s, he found glass fragments of Roman origin, pottery and iron. These he unearthed from behind the shop, where an old fireplace was also discovered. An archaeologist was certain that it dated back to the 13th or 14th century. Deeds of the property stated that before 1860 there were three cottages converted from an old pub called The Black Horse. Two-thirds of this is now 55 Head Street. The archway in the centre of the building on the left, was over a passageway that led to cottages in Chase Yard, until 1890 called Harrington's Yard, now demolished and a door has been fitted in the entrance. (See 91a)

91. Head Street in 1965

Behind the detached shop (centre) was Johnson's Yard, consisting of a few little old cottages, that stood between Head Street and Manfield. In 1890 the name was changed to Crown Yard after the "Rose & Crown" that stood nearby (92). Rose, the other half of the pub's name was given to a yard on the opposite side of the road, formerly Catley's Yard. The stone cottages on the left were demolished to make provision for the pub car park but after its closure the site was redeveloped with more houses.

91a Chase Yard

Many little yards of cottages were tucked away behind those lining Head Street such as - Burst, Chase, Rose, Catley's, Coates, Crown, Evans', Evans' Passage, Goodey's, School, Johnson, and Gilson's. The latter was named after a surgeon Dr Benjamin Gilson, who lived for a time at Blue Bridge House (3). He was a sport-loving man and kept greyhounds for coursing and to transport them had a special mahogany coach-built van made. He died in 1856 and the vehicle was sold. Over 70 years later it came to light still in use at a local farm, which speaks very highly of the maker and the materials he used.

92. Head Street, c1910

As you travel up Head Street this scene is very much the same, except the Rose & Crown is no longer a pub and the large building on the left has ceased to be a school. At the time the photo was taken the pub was very busy, especially on market days and on one such day a local solicitor with several others were caught drinking out of hours and heavily fined. At the latter end of its trading the name changed to the Gold Rush, eventually closing its doors in the 1980s and converted to housing. The school building has often been recorded as the old workhouse but I have found evidence that this was not so. Alice Porter, aged 94 years in 1925 recalled the 1830s when she states that the old workhouse was situated in Workhouse Lane (now Mill Chase), at the rear of the Greenwood School before being replaced by a larger building in Hedingham Road (111). She recalled that part of the Greenwood School premises was known as the Church Charity Schools, forerunner of St Andrew's Schools, the large building overlooking Head Street, recently converted into residential units. At the Church Charity School lessons were taught and on Wednesdays a basin of broth was served to those who went to school clean, the children taking their own bread. Alice's schooldays were few as she left at the age of eight years to go to work. The wisteria covered house in the centre, 93 Head Street, has been connected with the Veterinary service for about 200 years.

93. The former "Napier Arms", Head Street

At the time this photo was taken the building was the Napier Arms, having been a pub for about a hundred years. Before that a veterinary business was established by William Wallis in 1810. He was succeeded by his son William Sheppard Wallis in 1836, who continued until the house was destroyed by fire. The family then had to move into rented accommodation until new premises were found. Eventually the buildings opposite were purchased, a forge and two cottages which stood in line with the neighbouring properties. A Georgian front section was added in 1854 making one large house, now 93 Head Street. The forge at the rear had been in use since the 16th century. William gradually built up the veterinary practice which after his death in 1892 was carried on by his son, Frederick Morton Wallis. Fire almost destroyed their livelihood again in 1918 when a fire left burning in the office to warm an adjoining fernery, ignited some clothing left to dry. Although the heat was intense and much damage was sustained in those two rooms, the fire was contained, being the old part of the house built with substantial materials that withstood the fire. The practice carried on but began to get rundown during the following years as Frederick was more interested in local affairs. He was forced to retire due to poor health and this is when Wilfred Waters stepped into the 'harness' (95).

The building standing at the junction of Head Street and Morley Road, seen on the right, was formerly the home of Miss Jarman, who was an objector to the Waterworks being set up nearby in 1862 (70). She was obviously upset by the decision as she sold her house to the Guardians of the Union, who adapted it for the Registrar's office in May of that year. The house remained in the Council's possession until 1924 and is now a hairdressers.

94. The old Fire Station, Head Street in 1966

This area next door to Napier House (93) was once the Urban District Council Offices and yard, the office being the small lean-to on the right near the entrance. In 1897 a cart horse was purchased for £63 but it was too big for the dilapidated cart, so a new tumbril had to be obtained as well. The horse, said to be the largest in the area, pulled the watercart round the town spraying the streets to lay the dust in the Summer and many other jobs where lorries are used today. He must have outgrown his living quarters too, as new stables and a cart shed were erected at the end of the yard, later becoming the Fire Station until transferring to new premises in Parsonage Street in 1968. This building is a private residence today. The original Surveyor's office had a new room added in 1911, costing £15 because when he was interviewing people on private matters, the clerk had to stand outside in the street. Halstead had its own Volunteer Fire Brigade, many of them local business men, formed in 1878. In 1921 an argument broke out with the Council resulting in the resignation of all the Volunteers, a band of dedicated men, who had given great service to the town for nearly half a century. Situated in the wall to the left of the entrance one can see a rare King Edward VII post box.

95. Wilfred Waters, Veterinary Surgeon

Wilfred Waters was born in Norfolk in 1885, qualified as a vet in 1907 and bought a practice in Blofield, near Norwich. At that time horses were part of every farm and were essential to business. Delivery men such as butchers, bakers, milkmen, greengrocers, in fact people in all walks of life relied upon the horse. For this reason most of Wilfred's patients were of the equine variety. In 1915, during the War, he enlisted, first being sent to France where he was in charge of the surgical ward in No. 2 Veterinary Hospital in Le Havre. Here he carried out ten operations a day, mainly removing shrapnel. He transferred to the front line at Ypres and later to Palestine where he was in charge of 500 horses on the boat to Alexandria. After his demobilisation he returned to Blofield but the practice he left no longer existed, much to Halstead's gain as he came to the town and took over the Wallis practice in Head Street on January 1st 1920. In spite of countless kickings and knocks this grand old gentleman completed 68 years as a vet and lived to be 91 years.

96. 103 Head Street, c1908

When this photo was taken, the shop was No. 43 Head Street but is now No. 103 as the whole street was renumbered. It was a Grocer's and Baker's shop for many years with the bread being freshly baked at the rear by Frank Rayner and sold to the customers in the shop by his wife Ethel. Around 1800 the building was a public house called The Bold Robin Hood with an adjoining wheelwright's workshop where years later I made my first attempt at milking a cow. Strangely enough the area ended its commercial life as Head Street Dairy - nothing to do with my earlier effort I'm sure!

FROM

F. RAYNER,

GROCER AND BAKER,

43, HEAD STREET, HALSTEAD,

LUNCHEONS AND TEAS PROVIDED.

Flour of the Finest Quality. Cakes made to Order.

HEDINGHAM ROAD formerly NORTH STREET

97. Hedingham Road entrance during the 1880s

Standing on the corner of a very narrow Hedingham Road, then North Street, is the London & County Bank which transferred its business to the present National Westminster Bank further down the High Street in 1915. During the same year the empty building served as a War Hospitals Supply Depot, where a ladies working party met twice a week for the purpose of making bandages and swabs, urgently required by the Military & Naval Hospitals. This continued until 1917 when Mr G.S. Morton, solicitor, purchased the redundant bank for his office. The shop in the centre is now on the corner, as the former bank and cottages behind were demolished in 1927 when the road was widened. It is recorded that this building was the birthplace of Elizabeth Holmes in 1706, a very charitable lady and it was her wish that after her death her body should stand in front of it. Her body arrived from London during the night and stood before this house until an hour before her burial in 1783. She is buried in a family vault in St Andrew's churchyard. There is a large marble tablet on the north wall of the church displaying the particulars of her will.

98. Stanley Moger, O.B.E.

George Stanley Murray Moger, known as Stanley, an auctioneer and estate agent, came to Halstead in 1892, acquiring the business of Messrs Bentall and Robinson at 23 High Street (138), before moving to his own office at 4 North Street during World War I. He soon became connected with the development of the Beridge Estate and was responsible for the opening up of Beridge Road, which replaced a footpath leading over the existing Common to Slough Farm, shortly followed by Stanley Road which took his name. He was first elected onto the Urban Council in 1898, serving for three years. He was voted on again in 1914 where he remained until his death in 1947, aged 76 years. He helped in the community in many ways and his efforts were rewarded in 1937 when he received the Order of the British Empire for his public and political services. He served as a Special Constable for over 15 years and was made Inspector in charge of the Halstead & Hedingham Division, for which he was awarded the King's Medal for the Special Police and was also Adjutant of the 2nd Volunteer Batt. of the Essex Regiment. He is remembered as a man who helped many people and his thought for others and the community was shown in his will where he made provision for the Urban Council to have the option of purchasing the Queen's Hall for £1,000.

99. The King's Arms in 1965

Now a private residence, this pub was once the King's Arms, an old building said to have been the Ostler's Tap of an inn with the same name in the High Street (135). During 1973, when Malcolm and Diana Peglar were carrying out renovations, coins dating back to George III and beyond were found under the floorboards. Eliza Cook and her son, Sid, consecutively held the licence of the pub for 51 years until 1952. In the early 1920s Sid commenced a birch broom business there with the help of Walter Drury of Pump Yard. The Drury family were well known in the broom-making industry. Walter's father Henry and his uncle Absolam of Box Mill were both in the trade and during the early 1900s Henry walked to Gosfield every day to work for Golden Jeggo, who had a flourishing business and lived in half of what is now known as Broom Cottage, with his wife and ten children. Here the men sat on the dirt floor making brooms with locally grown birch twigs. For a few years Walter had a break, when he went to be "Boots" at the George before joining Sid in his venture. Walter's brother James was a champion broom maker, turning out eighteen an hour. After the pub's closure, it served for a while as the local headquarters of the St John's Ambulance.

100. Hedingham Road pre 1951

Hardly recognisable today is Hedingham Road before redevelopment of this corner in 1951. On the extreme left is Charlie Bragg's shop standing at the top of Upper Chapel Street. Charlie started his fruit business in the early 1900s, later adding confectionery and fish. For many years he was a familiar figure travelling all over the area with his pony and cart selling winkles. The shop, with all but two of the cottages, was demolished about 1960. At the other end of the row was a passageway leading to Belle Vue Terrace and on the right of this was the old Boar's Head, a beerhouse run by William Cook (103) until about 1880 when another pub with the same name opened just round the corner in Upper Chapel Street, which was almost certain to have been built by William himself. This one became a private residence in 1930 after its closure when the licence was withdrawn due to all the other licensed premises in the neighbourhood - within 400 yards there were eleven pubs and one beerhouse. The large house (right) was The Manse (102) and on the extreme right is part of yet another pub called The Fleece, thought to have traded until at least 1835, when Thomas Porter was landlord. Between these two buildings is Fleece Yard, said to have taken its name from the fact that fleeces were taken by this route for the weavers during the Bay and Say trade. In Fleece Yard a row of little dwellings, with no gardens stood between the roadway and the chapel. These were described as being dry, ventilated and in good repair, having just one room upstairs and down. They were chiefly occupied by single women living on slender means in the early 1900s, who wanted small houses requiring little heating for small rent. In spite of this a report says that in 1895 twenty people were living in one of them - I believe that is classed as overcrowding!

101. Hedingham Road Baptist Church, 1895

As you stand at the entrance to Elizabeth Way and look across the road today, you see a modern Baptist Church that replaced this one in 1967/8. In 1678, sixteen years after the Act of Conformity, Baptists separated from other non-conformists and built their own place of worship, probably hidden away further along the then Hedingham Lane. The Conventicle Act (1664) forbade more than four persons, in addition to the household, gathering for worship - transportation being a punishment for offenders. The same year saw the publication of *"Pilgrim's Progress"*, written by another Baptist, John Bunyan, whilst in Bedford prison, suffering 12 years for his beliefs.

During the ministry of the Rev. William Hallowbread 1788-1799, a piece of land and two cottages were bought on the site of the present church, when the cottages were transformed into a meeting house. Shortly after the minister died and was the first to be interred in the graveyard. The church in the photo was erected in 1816 during the ministry of Rev. John King 1808-1832, when the previous building became too small for increased congregations. The cost was £815 and half of this amount was raised by John himself by travelling around the county in a pony and trap conducting services on his way. For about a hundred years up to 1829 baptisms had taken place in the river at Box Mill. One day whilst preparing the usual venue the depth of water was too low, inspiring the idea of installing a baptistry in the chapel. By 1835 there were disagreements among the members resulting in the dissolution of the church. Most of them were readmitted but the rest "opened a cottage" - the start of the Providence Baptist Church. After 150 years the photographed chapel was overcome by the ravages of time and repair bills were too costly resulting in its demolition by voluntary labour. Today's church was erected with the help of a generous gift from Mr & Mrs A.E. Evans in memory of their youngest daughter Christine in 1968. Whilst without a church the Baptists held services in the Drill Hall, Pretoria Road (207).

102. North Street Baptist Church and Manse, c1850

The Manse was a house with a history that came to an end in 1951 when it was demolished, allowing a dangerous corner to be widened in Hedingham Road. In 1818 the Baptists erected the Manse on the site of two old cottages, one of which was a butcher's shop, from where meat was sold on Sundays much to the annoyance of the congregation. During the ministry of Rev. William Clements, who ran a college for young men, more room was required, so he purchased more cottages adjoining the back of the Manse in Fleece Yard, to extend it at his own expense. Consequently the entrance porch and two rooms up and down on the north side of the Manse belonged to him and the other half to the church. Eventually the latter acquired the whole building in 1886 and for the next 14 years it served as the minister's home. After then the ministers lived in rented accommodation until 1911 when East Lodge, Pretoria Road was purchased. The old Manse continued to be used for Sunday School work and the Young Men's Institute, formed in 1906 by Harry Hughes, having an average attendance of 50 young men on Sunday afternoons. This was balanced by an equal number of young women meeting at the same time in three classes forming the Young Women's Institute, held in a red brick building, built by William Clements, formerly used by "The Teetotallers" and known as the Hall of Science. Access to this was gained up a flight of steps from Fleece Yard and later became the Sunday School classrooms. During World War II the old Manse was occupied by the Military who left it in a bad state and only fit for storage purposes.

103. William Cook (1824-1911)

William Cook was born in 1824 and came to Halstead in 1847 from Gloucestershire. He was a beerhouse keeper and coal & timber merchant on land which was bought under the terms of the Colne Valley & Halstead Extension Act of August 13th 1859 for the railway. His property included many tenements, all occupied, as well as his own extensive house that once belonged to Wm. Martin, a charitable gentleman of the 1500s. This area became the station platform, railway buildings and forecourt. After he had sold the land he moved to North Street (Hedingham Road) where he ran a beerhouse called The Boar's Head, until this was converted into cottages about 1880 and another pub, with the same name erected round the corner in Upper Chapel Street, now a private house. He then became a housebuilder erecting about 130 houses, mostly three-bedroomed terraced properties - Belle Vue, Globe Yard, Kings Road, Garden Terrace, 25-39 Parsonage Street, Summers Row and Trinity Square plus several detached residences, which he let. To encourage his tenants to keep his properties in good decorative order he had a warehouse stocked with paint and wallpaper at 1d (½p) per roll, and all the visiting tenants were offered a free pint of his own draught beer. He could neither read or write yet became a prosperous businessman enabling him to help others by lending money. He was a well respected man, a staunch Liberal and a Unitarian, but did not take part in public affairs. He died in 1911 at Balham House, Upper Chapel Street, a house he built for himself. According to his granddaughter, the late Edith Staines, the house was built in the year when some notorious murders took place in Balham, London, and since the name was on everyone's lips he thought it would be very recognisable and useful in a business sense.

104. The Manor House by Morton Mathews

As some old cottages owned by S.A. Courtauld were being demolished in 1928, it was suggested that they were a converted wing of the original structure of Abels Manor. Morton Mathews, a local schoolmaster and artist, took up a challenge and from what he saw, produced this drawing of how he thought it had looked. Abels Manor had stood in Hedingham Road since at least the 13th century. Obviously it appeared run down to Holman in the early 1700s as he described it as no way being fit for a gentleman. A sketch of Halstead dated c1750 depicts the manor with a large walled garden. About this time it was used as a forerunner of a police station where manorial courts were held. Later it was converted into three or four dwellings with yards of small cottages at the rear. All this was demolished and replaced by Sense & Sensibility. One of the last residents, Rose Mortimer, related to me that as a young girl she lived with her family in the left side, which was still referred to as Abels. She slept in a little room in the gable end and remarked with a shiver how spooky it was. Also, an elderly lady drew me a sketch of how the area was in the late 1800s. At the extreme left stood the old Boar's Head, where a gap between this and the manor led to Belle Vue. The doorway in the centre was made into a passageway leading to Pump Yard, a cobbled courtyard. The gap between the right-side and cottage took one through to Well Yard and between the Dog and the last cottage was Dog Yard (107). Samuel Courtauld had all this area demolished replacing it with distinctive Tudor style houses. When the old Boar's Head was being converted into cottages in 1915, an old doorway was revealed after plaster had been removed from the studwork of the wall and the character of the mouldings gave an indication that the building was from the end of the 1400s. An old neighbour of the time remembered this and recalled that years later some old tapestries were found in vaults underneath - where are they now? During the early

1960s, when some cottages were pulled down in Belle Vue, at the rear of the old pub, there was considerable interest since this site was also believed to be the spot on which part of the old manor stood. Although the premises had been rebuilt several times constant rebricking and plastering had not hidden the evidence of centuries old building methods.

105. Washing day in the early 1920s

In the days before automatic washing machines, Dorcas Edwards had to do her laundry in a tin bath using water from a tap in the back yard. Her husband, Reuben (left) was the town crier for a time and used to practice ringing his bell and 'crying' in his home, much to the annoyance of his family and neighbours. Dorcas and Reuben were the grandparents of Rose Mortimer and are seen here behind their home in part of Abells Manor (104). Between their home and the old Boar's Head was an alleyway leading to Belle Vue where there was a door that was never opened. Rose and her friends wondered what secret was hidden behind it so inquisitively peeped through the keyhole. They saw more than they bargained for and ran away screaming thinking they had seen a dead man slumped in a chair. Further investigations revealed that the 'body' was "Rocky" Bragg's guy waiting for November 5th. When Abells Manor was demolished the family was re-housed in the newly built "Orville", Mallows Field, one of the Courtauld houses that had replaced Knaves Acre Row, said to have been the tallest weaver's cottages in the town.

106. Dog Yard, off Hedingham Road, c1900

Tucked away behind the houses in Hedingham Road, before demolition, was this part of old Halstead called Dog Yard. Access was through a narrow passageway beside the Dog (107), winding its way down to run parallel with Well Yard, situated off to the right of this photo behind the vegetation. It was there that Henry (Harry) Pavey Weston had his engineer and millwright's business. The ladies enjoying a neighbourly chat in the background are believed to be Suzanne Beadle and Mrs Curtis. Some of the yards off the Hedingham road in the 1800s were Boar's Head, Pump, Well, Dog, Valley, Fleece, Ivy, Balls, Cooks and George.

107. Part of Dog Yard, off Hedingham Road, c1900

This photo of a "bit of old Halstead" was taken c1900 and shows the condition of the dwellings that some families had to endure. Fifty years before many of the houses in Hedingham Road were referred to as just hovels, where the labouring classes had to live. They were for the most part small, badly constructed and in a filthy condition. There were clusters of cottages built back to back where overcrowding prevailed and disease was rife. For instance, in one of them 14 people were occupying two bedrooms with eight of them sleeping on the floor when typhus broke out. The Local Board of Health came into being in 1852 and in the following years great progress was made in sanitation for which we must all be thankful. The lady in the photo is standing in the passageway that led to Dog Yard (106) from the then North Street.

108. Hedingham Road during the 1940s

With the exception of the baker's shop (the first building on the left) all the other old houses were demolished circa 1950 for a road widening scheme. The bakery was once part of a former pub, The Rising Sun, closed in 1907 and is now a private residence, aptly called Sunbeam House. James Scott, when he died in 1901, had been in business in the town for 50 years and for 40 of these held the licence of the Rising Sun. He also carried on the bakery connected with it. His son, James, continued with the family tradition when he became the landlord of the Boar's Head (100) for a time at the turn of the 20th century. He later took on the job of bill-poster in Halstead and the neighbourhood until his death in 1923.

Between the shop and the next house was the entrance to Ivy Yard, previously called Balls Yard until 1890. The cottages in the background on the right, remain today as Sized Up and Luigi's restaurant. No. 11 Hedingham Road was formerly the saddlery and harness maker's shop of John Harvey, who traded in the town for nearly 60 years. When the use of horses diminished he turned his hand to mending shoes and footballs.

109. Vine House in the late 1800s

This fine double-fronted residence, Vine House, was the home of the Weston family for many years. Harry Weston, the son of a master builder responsible for the erection of several well-known bridges in Devon, came to Halstead from Colyton in 1872. He accompanied Mr Symington of Cardiff, who took over premises to revive a "sleeping" industry - the Colne Valley Ironworks - a foundry that was later taken over by Huggins & Atterton, then Archibald Smith & Co, followed by Portways. After ten years Harry commenced his own engineer and millwright's business off North Street and in that capacity visited practically all the mills and engineering works in this part of the county, repairing several old windmills that were demolished between 1880 and 1915. He married a daughter of James Scott, a baker and beer retailer at the Rising Sun (108). They had four daughters and nine sons, five of them serving in World War I. His mother was an excellent linguist and was buried in Petrograd, Russia. His sister Edith, also lived there before returning to England in 1921 after 48 years of teaching English to the Bolsheviks, with her sister, who had previously been an interpreter in Berlin before moving to Moscow. Vine House stood opposite the Dog, known many years ago as The Dog & Partridge. Another old pub, The Duke's Head, stood near the entrance to Mill Chase and is mentioned in a sale notice when the area was all old cottages. Vine House was demolished in the 1920s to make way for "Persuasion", one of the Courtauld houses. The gateway to the right of the house was the entrance to cottages in Vine Yard.

110. North Street, c1900

In quieter days before juggernauts and fast cars, this was the narrow North Street before redevelopment by Samuel Courtauld in the 1920s. The gabled end house on the right stood next door to The Dog and was demolished to widen the road after which "Emma", the mock Tudor house was set further back from the road as were the other Courtauld houses that replaced all the cottages on the opposite side. All that remains are the terraced houses, 46-60 Hedingham Road, erected on the site of three old cottages in 1879, a few years before the establishment of the Cottage Hospital nearby. A committee was formed but it seemed an impossible task as land had to be purchased before one could be built that would have to be furnished and maintained. The first two hurdles were overcome when George Courtauld purchased an acre of land from John R. Vaizey, off North Street on April 11th 1883, offering to build the hospital in memory of his second wife Susannah. Pledges of support were received from many people including £20 from Mrs Johnson towards the cost of a bed in memory of her husband Benjamin Johnson (151). An out-patients block was added in 1920 as a memorial to George Courtauld and in 1968 The League of Friends of Halstead Hospital was formed, raising much needed money to provide services and facilities to keep the hospital for the people of the town and surrounding area. A new hospital and nursing home completed in 1993 were built at the rear of the original hospital which still serves the community.

111. The Workhouse in Hedingham Road in 1882

Workhouses were built throughout the country under the 1728 Act and Essex had more than other counties. The original Halstead workhouse was established around 1733 on the site of the old Greenwood School (177) in Mill Chase, then called Workhouse Lane. Most of the residents, in the late 1700s were women and three outside cottages accommodated widows. In 1803 the women were occupied in spinning, raising £52 to help pay for their bed and board. The building had 17 rooms, a communal dining room, a large ward, washing room, as well as other rooms and a nursery. By 1794 about 30 poor people were housed there at a cost of 2/3d (11p) per week. Those who were resident were classed as receiving 'indoor' relief as opposed to those acquiring 'outdoor', who received help from the Parish in return for carrying out more manual work within the parish, such as carpentry and property repairing enabling those with homes to stay in them rather than becoming inmates when the whole family would be taken in but separated. Those receiving 'indoor' relief were usually orphans, incapacitated, elderly, infirm or widows.

Dominating the skyline in 1882 was the Workhouse built in 1838 to replace the smaller one in Workhouse Lane, now Mill Chase. About 400 destitute people of all ages could be housed there, including tramps, who were only allowed to stay for one night and before leaving had to perform a menial task. One tramp, unhappy with the breakfast provided for him, refused to carry out his task of picking 4lb. of oakum. For his refusal he was sentenced to seven days hard labour. Oakum was loose hemp or jute used to make rope, sometimes treated with tar or creosote for caulking (making watertight) seams in wooden ships. In 1881 there were just over 100 inmates, over half of them had been connected to the Agricultural or

Strawplaiting industries and had become destitute due to the decline. The field seen opposite the workhouse was kept as a kitchen garden by the inmates for self-support, with fruit trees at the bottom reached by a nasturtium lined path running down the centre. Several local influential people often treated the less fortunate and one of them, George Courtauld, used to transport residents to his home at Cut Hedge, Gosfield, where he provided them with tea on the tennis lawn. He smoked a pipe with the men, giving them all tobacco and pipes, presented the women with sweets and biscuits and each child received a present. January 1st 1909 proved to be a happy new year for thousands over the age of 70, as they were able to go to the post office for the first time to draw their weekly pension of 5/- (25p). Happily there was a drop in the number at workhouses and in 1916 the remaining 53 at Halstead were transferred to Kedington. Miss K. Courtauld, of Colne Engaine, lent her ambulance for the bedridden, motor cars were hired and covered waggonettes chartered for the 15 mile ride through the pretty countryside - a treat for most of them. The War Office occupied the old workhouse as a compound for German prisoners of war in February 1918. These men worked on local farms and were sent in gangs of six, under the charge of a British guard, many travelling by train each day to the Hedingham and Yeldham areas. After Peace was declared a crowd of 244 singing Germans marched through the town in October 1919, on their way back home, many vowing to return. What would happen to the workhouse now? There were suggestions like converting it to palatial accommodation for a number of families, a social centre or a mat factory. The outcome was its purchase by Samuel Augustine Courtauld followed by demolition, at a time when there were 280 men unemployed and 80 of these were given jobs here in 1922/3 under the charge of S.G. Woodman. There were many sales of the enormous amount of building materials. A large quantity of bricks was offered for the erection of St Andrew's Hall, Parsonage Street, and it was hoped to reserve enough to build the almshouses that were built on the site (112). Windows, doors etc found their way into buildings around the town and many lorry loads of brick rubble were purchased by Clacton Urban Council for road making.

In 1923 the Board of Guardians received a cheque for payment of the sale of the workhouse, when it was proposed that the money would be used to build the new office and boardroom in Colchester Road (60).

For those in workhouses life was very hard, living under masters who were virtually free to do as they liked with them, resulting in many dying of neglect or starvation. Halstead's workhouse was different - it was the centre of a Poor Law Union embracing 17 parishes and was acknowledged by the authorities to be one of the best managed and most up to date in the country.

112. Residents of the Homes of Rest in 1948

The redundant workhouse (111) was bought by Samuel Courtauld to demolish and provide a site where he could build 20 homes to benefit the town. He visited many homes of rest in various parts of the country to find out what type of house was best suited for the older person. The Homes of Rest were ready for occupation in 1924 and to qualify for one, persons had to have either worked or resided in the town for at least 25 years and to have a "good character for honesty, sobriety and steady work". Former employees of Courtauld's Halstead factory were given preferential consideration. The homes were suitable for single people, married couples or friends sharing. The first residents to move into the 20 homes, arranged in five blocks of four houses, presented a Malacca walking stick, with an engraved gold band, to Mr S.A. Courtauld and his wife received a lizard skin card case, to mark their combined gratitude to their generous benefactor. Twenty-five years later there were 29 people living there with a combined age of 2,065 years, many of them having worked at the factory. Kate Godfrey had 30 years service, Harriet & Mary Cressall 35 and 32 years respectively. Mrs Reeve, with 38 years service, used to walk to and from Belchamp Otten everyday, and Eliza Kensall walked in all weathers from The Thatch, Greenstead Green to the factory starting work at 6 am, sometimes through deep snow and floods for 45 years. The photo was taken on the steps in front of the bay window of the Common Room. This is a fine oak-panelled room in the middle of the centre block, used as a common room or room for Trustee's meetings. For many years these were held at Red House (64). The people in the photo are:

Front Row : Minnie Smith, Fred Meadows, Mr Gaymer and his daughter Beattie.

Back Row : Miss Woolmer, Ernest Layzell, Mrs Mead, Mary Meadows, Mary Cressall, Mrs E Reeve, Ethel Constable, Kate Godfrey and Lydia Monk.

113. Hedingham Road in the early 1900s

This quiet scene, free from traffic, is now the busy A1124 and at the time the photo was taken, was affectionately called Emma Sly's corner after an old lady living in this part of the then North Street. The first six cottages on the left and all the others on the right were pulled down in the early 1920s at the same time the Workhouse (111) suffered the same fate. The large wall on the right was the front boundary of this institution. The year before the Workhouse was opened, was the Coronation of Queen Victoria and for the occasion 4,000 inhabitants of Halstead received 1lb. of meat and 2d (1p) to celebrate the happy event in their own homes, the sum of £141 having been subscribed. To meet the demand 60 sheep were slaughtered. The population at the time was about 5,000. The church was decorated and the streets lined thickly with firs, oaks etc, which gave the appearance of long avenues of trees.

114. The Anchor Inn, 89 Hedingham Road, c1960

"The Rising Sun scorched The Dog and made the Boar's Head fly,
Turned the King's Arms inside out and drank the Anchor dry."

These five pubs plus The Fleece were all at one time in Hedingham Road. One by one they have closed leaving only The Dog trading today. Here we see The Anchor, 89 Hedingham Road, that began life as a beerhouse. The first mention of this property that I could find was in 1850 when Thomas King was referred to as a beer retailer, as were his successors until 1934 when the name Anchor came into being. James Patrick and his wife Elizabeth held the licence for over 30 years with James carrying on a general haulage business from the rear. In 1937 Charles William (Toots) Argent took over the pub complete with a dozen iron spittoons and bought the haulage business including "Betty" an old bay mare and "Captain", a six year old chestnut gelding. When "Toots" started, the payment for a day's work carting manure for Miss Adams, of Oaklands, was 12/6d (62½p) - that was the horse, cart and man. Most work was done for the Halstead Gas Company transporting coal from the Railway to the Gasworks in Rosemary Lane. After the coal had been processed, he then delivered the resulting coke for heating purposes to customers all over the town and surrounding area, especially schools, churches, hospitals and businesses. In 1941 he started transporting Fremlin's beer from the brewery (236), by horse and cart, travelling many miles to local and village pubs, always accompanied by his dog who ran ahead and waited patiently for them at the next port of call. "Toots" left the Anchor in 1943 to work for Fremlin's as a drayman. The Anchor closed its doors on June 29th 1969 and is now a private house.

115. Cottages at The Wash, c1900

At the opening of St Andrew's Hall in 1924, Samuel Augustine Courtauld declared that "it was very pleasant for him as a Halstead man, to see it take the place of the mean, ugly little structure which formerly stood on the site" and "anything that would improve the mean, ugly and squalid buildings in Halstead, and improve the town, must have the hearty support of all townspeople." These sentiments resulted in Samuel buying up properties to demolish, that he found offensive to himself and his visitors as they drove to his home at The Howe (118). Many were situated in Hedingham Road and were replaced by the familiar Courtauld Tudor styled houses, all bearing the SAC monogram, date and a name. Mr Courtauld was a great novel reader and all the house names are based on some of his favourites. In Hedingham Road we have "Sense & Sensibility", "Emma", "Pride & Prejudice", "Persuasion", "Northanger Abbey" and "Mansfield Park", titles of Jane Austen's books. The houses in Colchester Road, "Fanny Burney", "Duval", "Branghton" and "Mirvan", with "Orville", and "Evelina" in Mallows Field, commemorate characters in "Evelina" by Miss Fanny Burney, born 1752, a diarist and novelist, whose diaries began in 1768, continuing for more than 70 years and were a witty, sophisticated and stylish record of the manners of the polished English society of her day. At the age of 34, Fanny became Second Keeper of the Robes to Queen Charlotte. The houses that replaced the cottages in the photo, take the names of old Halstead families, Bousser, Tryon, Martin and Clare. These were built behind the cottages, which were demolished after the occupiers had taken up residence in the new. This part of Hedingham Road, formerly North Street and Henningham Lane, was once called Blackenham Street.

116. The old Howe School, Hedingham Road, c1980

Standing at the Hedingham Road/Box Mill Lane junction is a house that was erected in 1861 by Edward Hornor, as a school, lecture and mission room for "use of that part of the parish near his seat at The Howe (118)", closing about 1880. There is also reference to a Howe School from 1816-1822, accommodating 122 pupils, with an average attendance of only 64 boys, but its whereabouts is unknown - probably on the same site. The welfare of others less fortunate than themselves was always foremost in the Hornor's thoughts and during the Lancashire Cotton famine the whole family went without sugar and were allowed a small sum of money each week in lieu of it. This money mounted up so that they were able to send £1 per week to the famine fund during its existence. In November 1891 they also opened a club from 7-9 pm at the old school. The club was intended for many working girls living in lodgings or over-crowded cottages, where they had to seek their recreation outdoors. Before the club had even opened 130 girls had applied for membership, the maximum permitted. They were taught singing, needlework and drawing as well as playing games and being entertained. After the demise of the club, the old school was used as a laundry before being converted into a private house.

117. Wash Cottages, Hedingham Road, c1900

This narrow country lane is now the A1124 and the charming pair of lath and plaster tiled roofed cottages stood at the top of Wash Hill, near to the present day entrance to Ashlong Grove. They consisted of one large living room each, fitted with a cooking range. The one on the left had a small scullery with copper, sink and water tap and two bedrooms. The other was the same but had the added luxury of a sitting room. Unfortunately they were demolished in 1922 by S. Courtauld when four new houses were erected in Box Mill Lane to replace these and two others that stood in Hedingham Road at the top of the Lane (115).

Ashlong Grove took its name from two men who were instrumental in the small development in the mid 1900s. Mr Van Ash, a property developer bought the Howe (118) from the Courtauld family and the solicitor who acted for him was Mr A.R. Long, of Wayman & Long, Clare. A combination of both their names resulted in Ashlong Grove.

118. The Howe, Hedingham Road, c1900

William Holman refers in his manuscripts written from 1700-1730 to the Hoo or How as a farm "of arable and pasture grounds lying on each side of the road leading from Halstead to Hipworth Hall", but "where the mansion house stood I find not." During those years it belonged to Robert Tweed, passing on to his daughter, who married John Whalley. William J Evans records about 1886, in *Old and New Halstead* that Edward May built the present house, but whether he demolished an earlier one is not known. Edward bought the Howe estate from John Sparrow in 1825, presumably as a country seat. He was the youngest son of John May of Claverings, Greenstead Green, where his descendants still live today. Edward had an ironmongery business in Oxford Street, London, but sadly did not retire to Halstead as he died in London at an early age. His eldest daughter caused quite a stir in 1834 when she eloped from the Howe with a 35 year old local solicitor. Her furious father followed in hot pursuit to Gretna Green, but alas arrived too late. Mr & Mrs Edward Hornor took up residence at the Howe in 1845, a Quaker family from Yorkshire. Edward, a Justice of the Peace, had the school (116) built at the bottom of Wash Hill, where his daughters carried on excellent work. When the school closed educational evening classes were run by his daughter Florence and friends. She was born at the Howe where she lived over 60 years but after the death of her mother in 1914 she moved to Red House (64). In her early years she was a member of the Society of Friends (Quakers) but later joined St Andrew's Church. Samuel A. Courtauld then purchased the Howe which remained in his family's possession until 1955 when a firm of estate developers bought it and sold off much of the grounds for high quality houses that line the drives to the Howe.

119. Esther Cockerton

Like many young girls of her era Esther Cockerton went into domestic service after she left school at a very young age. She was born in 1874 at Gosfield and when old enough she became a domestic kitchen-maid for Robert Rutherford Morton at Star Stile during the 1880s, transferring to the Howe, where she worked for the Hornor family until her marriage, in 1899, to William Botham of Halstead. Here we see her dressed in her maid's outfit at the Howe.

120. Brownie Pack, 1924

The Hornor and Courtauld families were very generous in allowing their spacious grounds at The Howe to be used by local people for garden parties, Sunday School treats etc. The young girls in this photo, outside the summerhouse, were the Brownies, taken in 1924 when Mrs Courtauld had invited them for tea. When the junior section of the Girl Guides was formed in 1914 they were called "Rosebuds", but the name was not very popular. A year later they were renamed "Brownies" after Lord Baden-Powell read a book entitled "The Story of the Brownies" by Mrs Ewing.

Front Row, l to r : Ivy Cooper, Doris Burl, Lily Cooper, Milly Burl.

2nd Row : Hilda Snowden, Edna Kibble, Norah Curtis, Rose Edwards, Mrs Saunders, Eleanor Binks, Eva Tansley, Lennox Kibble, ?, Ivy Arnold.

3rd Row : Doris Arnold, Emily Abbott, ?, Gwen Pogson, Doris Hume, Ivy Clift, Winnie Edwards, Marjorie Berry, Norah Wicker, Rosie Clark, Connie Baker.

Back Row : Mary Norfolk, Winnie Reynolds, Flo Reeve, Violet Abbott, Ena Button, Ada Davey, Dora Wicker and Ivy Harrington.

121. The Howe Cottages, Hedingham Road

Taking a walk along the Hedingham Road before the 1930s you would have been greeted with this scene on the bend just past Howe Chase. All these cottages were for the estate workers of The Howe (118). The pair in the foreground were demolished in the 1930s and the stone cottages, standing at right angles to the road suffered the same fate 30 years later. Behind these stood the clubhouse of the Golf Club and older Halsteadians still refer to the fields in that area as the Golflinks. At that time the road from the top of Wash Hill (117) to Does Corner (123) was lined with elm trees, all succumbing to Dutch Elm Disease in the early 1970s.

The energetic golfers of the district had a course near the town well over a century ago. Dr C.G. Roberts established a club at Blamster's Farm before 1897 but in that year the members agreed to transfer the links to its "old locale" at Fitzjohn's Farm, near Does Corner, implying that they had been there before. The area was said to have light soil that permitted play all the year round and was situated near Bennett's Park. The course was in use for about 20 years before being relocated near the main road between Does Corner and The Howe. This nine hole course covered 27 acres and with an annual subscription of £1 1s (£1.05) for ladies and £2 2s (£2.10) for gentlemen, encouraged 60-70 members to join within a few months. During the Essex Show at The Howe in 1924, the golf-links were set out for the parking of cars - at least 1,000 were catered for.

122. Fitzjohn's Farm off Hedingham Road

In 1933 the club suffered financial difficulties and had to make cuts in the expenditure resulting in a decision to dispense with the assistant green-keeper's services. Things did not improve so two years later the green-keeper was replaced by a lad receiving volunteer help from the committee. The club struggled on but the condition of the course deteriorated, being made worse by straying cattle from an adjoining field and burrowing rabbits causing havoc. The determined members carried on until 1945 when the course became unplayable due to labour shortage. A discussion was held the following March to terminate the tenancy but in May of that year the course was re-opened as more labour came forward. A fresh start was made after a very wet Summer and Autumn but after all the troubles and set backs a final decision was made to close the club on March 15th 1948.

123. Does Corner, Hedingham Road, in the late 1800s

The Local Board of Health considered converting these cottages at Does Corner into an Isolation Hospital for typhoid and smallpox sufferers, but this failed to materialise as "The Hole" (182) was used in preference. A dozen men and a number of horses and carts were employed in 1908, removing part of the garden to make the dangerous corner safer. Halstead played host to the Essex Agricultural Society's Show in 1924, on four adjoining fields of some 28 acres, on a gentle slope from Hedingham Road down to the river, part of the Howe Estate. Machinery and stock arrived by road and rail, and visitors alighting from the train were greeted by flags and decorations that festooned the station yard and all the shops and businesses. The weather was atrocious causing parts of the showground to be impassable to foot traffic, resulting in Pudney Peirson's quickly selling their complete stock of rubber boots.

by Ian Potts

124. Does Corner, c1900

This peaceful scene captured on camera circa 1900 was taken of an old gentleman with a young child resting on Hepworth Hall bridge. Does Corner is in the background with the cottages (123), seen in the previous photo, nestling beside the narrow tree-lined lane to Halstead, now the busy A1124. Preparation for the 1924 Essex Show included the demolition of the cottages and the widening of the corner. Also a mile of roadway was completely remade with tarmacadam in order that there would be none of the 'ruttiness and dust', as a great deal of traffic was expected.

125. Crested china bearing the old Halstead Arms

No Halstead seals that were placed on Bays and Says have ever been found but it has been suggested that the materials might have been stamped with the Royal Crown that for many years was used as the town Arms. It appears on many pieces of crested china and used as an emblem by the Halstead Chamber of Commerce, the old HUDC, and is featured on the Railway shield (208). At the beginning of the 1900s, a local historian described the Arms as of "doubtful authority", as Halstead had possessed no corporate body to bear Arms, but stated that the town once had a large and important Guild, with the Guildhall situated at the bottom of the High Street (166).

125a. Sketches of the Arms of Halstead

These sketches appear in Heraldry books. The one on the left shows the crown of Edward I (1272-1307) and is dated 1647. Berry, in his dictionary of Heraldry (1830) states that the Arms of Halstead are "a coronet of one fleur-de-lis and 2 leaves on the bend". A second reference is in *General Armoury* (1875) by Sir Bernard Burke describing it as "Azure, with a coronet composed of fleur-de-lis, and 2 leaves, Or" (right). Alfred Hills, historian, says of this information in the 1920s, that "Heraldic writers do not invent these things and other town's Arms are recorded accurately". He believed the drawings were made from an early seal which had been lost.

126. The Market House

This sketch of the old Market House that stood on the Market Hill was drawn by Morton Mathews from an old steel engraving of the High Street c1750. It is believed to have been built chiefly for the Bay and Say trade and was established circa 1561. During the 14th and 15th centuries the weaving trade grew and great fortunes were made in the area from the products of the cottage industry. The persecutions of Protestants by the Duke of Alva brought many Flemish weavers to this country, 30-40 families settling in Halstead in 1576, who at once began to use their weaving skills. Bay was a beautiful twill serge, with a soft nap raised by teasels, used for garments and stockings - the name coming from its red-brown tint before being dyed. The name survives today in baize, a green woollen material often used to cover snooker tables. Say was a thinner fabric and was used for linings and the green aprons worn by Quakers. Large quantities were exported for the making of habits for monks and nuns. Every roll was examined and only those that were perfect were put on the market with an attached lead ticket or seal - a guarantee of its quality. The locals were soon up in arms when the Dutch sealed material was sold for more money and they started to forge the seals to put on their own rolls. This practice upset the Dutchmen who packed their bags and left, resulting in a sharp decline in exports and much local distress. The foreigners were begged to return but never did. There was a post in the Market Place used for the 'sealing' of the fabrics, also ancient stocks and a whipping post. After the Dutch left the market continued to be used for livestock. It was reported in 1777 about a different sort of livestock sale. A master butcher from Halstead sold his wife to a wealthy farmer for a sum of 3 guineas (£3.15) and a good supper - the woman agreed to the bargain and the farmer immediately took her home well pleased with his purchase. During World War II, when normal office activities were greatly restricted, a series of Halstead Market grants dating from 1250 to 1531 were discovered in the cellar of a London solicitor's office. They were found when the box containing them was hauled down from a high shelf. The grant was made by King Henry III, on the 17th November 1250 to Abel de St Martin, the Lord of the Manor, permitting him to take for his own use the profits from tolls collected in the market held every 8th and 9th October. The Market House was removed in 1816, the upper floor was taken whole to serve as a cottage near The Common. The stocks were removed at the same time when people in the 1880s could remember a young lad being put in them to be whipped for stealing fruit from Bois Hall and an old man was whipped for stealing firewood.

126a. The Jubilee Fountain

To commemorate the Golden Jubilee of Queen Victoria's reign, George Courtauld generously contributed to the erection of the fine fountain in place of the obelisk. No doubt it was a boon in the early days, supplying the need of the thirsty. After an arduous trek up the hill horses could stop for a well earned rest to quench their thirst from the troughs whilst the humans partook of the water from the taps. Dogs were not forgotten and they too had small troughs underneath. With the decline of the use of horses the troughs were filled in and adorned with flowers.

127. The Market Hill between 1861 & 1887

Just two horse-drawn vehicles, two wheelbarrows and a few spectators appear in this scene of the Market Hill in the mid 1800s. The shops on the right were built in 1861 and the obelisk removed in 1887, dating the photo between those years. The Market House (126) was replaced in 1816 by the obelisk which in turn was removed in favour of the fountain to commemorate Queen Victoria's Golden Jubilee. Peace in this area was shattered during a period of unrest caused by the introduction of agricultural machinery. Workers gathered to protest against this and their extremely low wages. A riot broke out as the mob attempted to free four men arrested for destroying some machinery at Sible Hedingham. One of the constables conveying them to prison had to flee for his life and took refuge in a house, which was furiously attacked. The mob continued to make indiscriminate attacks on many shops and houses of principal inhabitants and the following evening greater numbers gathered, including men from neighbouring villages, many armed with cudgels. The Halstead Cavalry were under arms and the Riot Act was read. Several charges were made on the mob that retreated into the churchyard from where they bombarded the cavalry with stones. Early the next day a squadron of Dragoon Guards accompanied by 60 constables arrived from Colchester and fought their way into the battered town to join forces with "respectable tradesmen and residents." The situation was eventually brought under control.

On the left is the George Hotel, an old coaching inn, thought to go back to the reign of Queen Mary (1553-8), with its high passageway for access by horses and coaches. It was mentioned in the 1700s as one of the best inns in town with nine bedrooms. The George was closed at 9.15 pm on April 28th 1915 as a place where intoxicating liquors could be obtained, due to the licence being surrendered, but carried on for a while providing accommodation for travellers until being put up for auction on July 10th 1917 but not sold. A year later it became a soup kitchen for the benefit of large families, old age pensioners and infirm. Soup was one penny per pint on production of a jug and a ticket. A boiler and other utensils were supplied by H.H. Portway in which to make the soup and townsfolk supplied vegetables and money for the project. Lloyd's Bank then purchased and reconstructed the building, opening the Halstead branch in November 1920. The bank remained until moving down the High Street when Lloyd's amalgamated with the Trustees Savings Bank in 1999. After renovation the ground floor opened in August 2002 as Halstead Physiotherapy Clinic. To the right of the George is the Town Hall built in 1850 by a Company of speculating townsmen. The upper floor consisted of a large hall used for public meetings, concerts and lectures, with board meetings taking place in a smaller room. The ground floor was originally a corn exchange, later becoming the Literary & Mechanics Institute, used as a reading room and library for over 200 members. A century later interest gradually lessened with its inevitable closure in December 1930. The local Council then took over the property and after a long discussion on its further use, decided that a library would be beneficial. A branch of the Essex County Library opened the following year in the room previously used by the Institute. There were 600 books available, being changed every few months. After four years the old Town Hall was sold to the East Anglian Electric Supply Co., with arrangements being made to move the library to the Friends Meeting House (61) and the Council to Red House (64), both in Colchester Road. After the Electricity Board moved to new premises in Bridge Street the old Town Hall had many uses and is presently the CO9 Café Bar. An improvement took place on the Market Hill in 1861 when a block of buildings was constructed - the two large shops to the right of the Town Hall. They were for the business of Wm. Knight, a silversmith and Joseph and Robert Doubleday, grocer and draper, already trading in the area. Wm. Knight occupied a shop adjoining the Hall as far back as 1830 until 40 years later when Henry Knight took over. This business ended in bankruptcy in 1891 and a few weeks later a disastrous fire broke out and great efforts were made and succeeded in saving neighbouring buildings. Nearly as much water was deposited on the firemen from faulty hoses as on the fire, which proved to be a blessing as the intense heat caused the spray to rise as steam from their brass helmets, heated almost beyond bearing. The warehouses were completely destroyed at the rear. After restoration Richard Minter ran an ironmongery shop, followed by the well-known E.W. Cant (Ned) and his family. They were house furnishers "able to supply everything for the home with the exception of the baby". Ned started his business in 1924 at the rear of 21 High Street, moving down to the old ropeworks (214) before ending up on the Market Hill in 1937. Ned's daughter and son-in-law, Beatrice and Lloyd Rayner, ran the business with Ned taking an active interest until his death in 1976 aged 87 years. The shop was described as a step into Aladdin's cave, where treasures were arranged on three floors and differed from "a thimble to a three-piece suite, gold earrings to a coal-scuttle and carpets to Christmas wrapping paper". The Rayners retired in 1980 when the shop became Nettlefields.

128. The Market Hill, c1820

Yes, this is the top of the High Street, yet looks entirely different as there is an obelisk with gas lamps, Head Street is very narrow, with a 2-storey shop, Samuel Jesup's, standing on the corner and the church has a spire. The most interesting area is the row of buildings on the right. Part of it, with the many small paned windows was an inn called The Dolphin until 1759 and was of a considerable size, and note how narrow the entrance to Parsonage Street is. John Morley's (4) name was mentioned in the deeds and in the sketch there is an open-fronted butcher's shop - could this be where he started his trade? Compare this sketch with the next photo.

129. The Market Hill in the late 1850s

Years ago the entrance to Parsonage Street was extremely narrow and is said to have been widened during alterations to the church in the 1850s, when a cottage was demolished. If you compare this photo with the previous sketch (128) it is noticeable that the corner house is only half the width, with an extra storey added, allowing the road to be widened. The shop behind the obelisk and its neighbour was removed in 1861 and replaced by the large building we see today. The structure, with its unusual architecture and ornamental brickwork, was commended and the architect, Charles Hayward and Messrs Sudbury, builders of Halstead, who carried out the work, were highly praised by the Building News the following year. The little shop on the corner was a grocery and drapery run by Samuel Jesup and his son James, from the 1790s to 1841, when Joseph Doubleday took over the business with his brother. Twenty years later they moved into one of the new shops until 1897 when their nephews Edward and Thomas succeeded them. Before moving to Halstead Joseph had set up a grocery in Epping during 1760. He was a Quaker and kept in contact with William Pitt, the Prime Minister, who corresponded with a Friend (Quaker) in every county, in order to get first hand knowledge on such matters as the effects of taxation. In 1795 Pitt came to stay in the locality and was shown the dwellings of the poor in the town. He is said to have gazed in silent wonder and declared that he "had no conception that any part of England could present such a spectacle of misery." Three years before Pitt's visit, due to so much poverty, the Lying-In charity was formed. This Society loaned linen and gave gifts of baby clothes to those who could not afford to buy them. In 1863 trouble arose when some of the loaned articles were pawned but this did not cause the end of the Society as it was still functioning in 1893, when between 60-70 women were helped during the year. A great, great uncle of Joseph Doubleday sailed with the Pilgrim Fathers on the Mayflower and I was told that there is a painting in existence of him handing over some beans to Red Indians in exchange for land in New England to found the first Quaker settlement there.

130. Walter Clark's shop, 1 High Street

This corner shop, an eating place for many years, was for a long period connected to the furniture making trade and is said to have been founded on the site about 1750. The Oakley family traded here from the late 1700s, with Walter Clark joining them c1882, becoming the sole proprietor a decade later. The shop had extensive warehousing and workshops at the rear, where work of a very high standard was done. Due to this, Walter was commissioned by Samuel Courtauld to go on a Grand Tour of Europe, visiting Paris, Rome, Naples, Vienna and Florence. Whilst at the latter venue he had to visit a museum, make a drawing of a certain piece of furniture, then return to Halstead and reproduce it. The finished article contained over 6,000 pieces of inlay and took a long time to perfect. After Walter's death in 1918, his highly trained men carried on. People were amazed to see a beautiful oak dining-room suite, including a massive sideboard and 14 chairs exhibited in the shop, that had been designed and made on the premises from wood formerly part of an old windmill in Sible Hedingham.

Walter was a highly respected man and a churchwarden from 1899-1918 and to commemorate this an oak screen was made by his oldest employee, A. Davey and carved by S. Marshall, of Coggeshall, to the design of his son, Duncan Clark.

The screen, with four large panels carries the armorial shields of the Dioceses in which the parish has been at different times of its history - London, Rochester, St Albans and Chelmsford. Dedicated and presented in December 1919, it was placed in front of the singing gallery over the North porch in St Andrew's Church, where it remains today. Walter was known as "Perished of Cold" Clark, after his habit of rubbing his hands together as he discussed business with customers.

131. A man about his day's work in the 1940s

William Warren, a horseman at Slough Farm, Beridge Road, is seen here on his cart riding down the High Street. William's horse was negotiating the hill quite well in 1946 unlike the time twenty-one years earlier when the road was tarred, causing horses so much trouble that they had to be diverted into Parsonage Street and Mallows Field in order to transport their loads up and down the hill. William was the father of Frank Warren, a well-known landlord of the Essex Arms for many years. An unusual event took place here on the Market Hill in November 1907 - a tug of war between 30 local men and an elephant, the latter won. He was a member of a visiting circus.

132. When the Essex Show came to town in 1862

Halstead was transformed in 1862, by the decision of the Essex Agricultural Association to hold its first annual show at Sloe House (220). There was great excitement and much activity to decorate the town. New pavements were laid, house and shop fronts painted, flags, flowers and foliage hung from every available place. Arches and banners were displayed on business premises and across the main roads leading into town, bearing greetings such as Welcome, God Save the Queen, Strive & Win, Be not weary in Well Doing, The Earth is the Lord's, Peace & Plenty, Make Hay Whilst the Sun Shines and Success to Agriculture. A huge arch spanned the road near St Andrew's Church, designed by Mr J.H. Lee of the London & County Bank (97). It was surmounted by a large crown made with 1,800 roses by Rayner & Runnacles. A military bandstand and stage, seen on the left of the sketch, was temporarily erected as a two-storey construction over the causeway, bearing the inscription "Our Country's Defenders". This causeway was between 12 & 14 High Street before the alterations in 1865. After the show a grand firework display and dinner took place. A special train was arranged to leave the station at 9pm but was delayed, arriving late at Marks Tey, having managed to travel at a speed of nearly 7 mph - hardly the Flying Scotsman! The delay was probably due to the fact that there were 32 speeches after the dinner. The balance in hand after the show was £35 and it was suggested that this formed a nucleus of a fund for the erection of a handsome fountain on the Market Hill.

133. The High Street, c1860

Stand with your back to the Jubilee fountain and look down the street at the row of large buildings to the right - that same area is featured in this very early photo. The late Arthur Morgan, chemist of 12 High Street, related to me that Wm. Knight owned "Bleak House" on the right. Wishing to build larger premises, he asked permission from his neighbour to put some foundations on his property. This was granted with a charge of £1 per brick. Arthur could see the structure from his cellar, adding that it must have cost a small fortune as there were hundreds of bricks. Wm. Knight's large house is now Evans Shop and the bank, 14/16 High Street. Before rebuilding, in the days prior to the formation of the Police Force, offenders were arrested by the Parish Constable, then brought before the Bench held in the old building, a former Inn. Invariably the punishment ordered was flogging, carried out in the prison (20), administered with an instrument consisting of several wire lashes attached to a heavy wooden handle. According to the seriousness of the crime, from 12 strokes upwards were ordered. Some suffered from 30 to 40 for an offence which today would meet with just a caution or fine. When this punishment was abolished, the Bench decided to remind the public of it and hung the weapon on the outside of the prison as a warning. "Bleak House" was demolished in September 1865 by Harcourt Runnacles in preparation for the erection of the shop and dwelling house for Wm. Knight that we see today. Wm. E. Brown, a Quaker, came to Halstead in the 1840s as an apprentice to Mr Knight, whose business he ultimately acquired in 1870. He was a member of the Board of Guardians for over 40 years and a close friend of Lucy Greenwood (176), helping her in the founding of the Greenwood School (177). A.J. Brown (right) eventually became E. Ingle Wright.

134. The High Street, c1900

This photo was taken of a quiet, sleepy town with inquisitive children watching the cameraman, circa 1900. A survey taken in 1086 reveals that the right side was the sunny side where there were 22 timber dwellings thatched with reeds and rushes. For centuries gardens stretched down to an elder lined brook, which flowed down to the river from Paynter's Pond (70). A barrel arch was installed underground in the mid 1800s where the brick gully is. These gardens may account for the strip of land down the side of the street, used as a car park today and market place, still belonging to the Lord of the Manor. The shady side opposite was lined with "humble dwellings". The condition of the road in the photo leaves a lot to be desired and it is recorded that in 1853 about £250 was annually spent on roads of the whole parish, being £10 per mile. Picked stones were delivered on the roads at 2/6d (12½p) per load. Footpaths were mainly paved with round smooth pebbles known as "petrified kidneys" before the installation of pavement slabs. Many of the cottage floors were brick and a man rode round the town on a donkey cart selling sand to sprinkle on them.

135. Top of the High Street in the late 1800s

This photo illustrates how the "sunnyside" of the High Street was mainly large houses, before being divided into commercial premises with living accommodation above. The last one converted was No. 16, becoming a branch of the Midland Bank in 1966. An ancient building demolished to make way for Wm. Knight's house and shop in 1865, then called Bleak House (133), was once a hostelry. Way back, at least as far as 1666, it was called the Swan, changing to The King's Arms in the mid 1700s, and was still being advertised in a stagecoach travelling guide in 1803. Later John Baker, born in 1848, worked for both Wm. Knight and his successor Wm. Brown, completing 60 years service. During this time he chatted to "old greybeards" who could remember the King's Arms, with its entrance for coaches from the market place, stabling for the horses at the rear and a cobbled outlet into North Street (Hedingham Road), directly opposite another licensed premises called the King's Arms (99). The outlet is still there but the cobbles have been covered up. The two dwellings, Nos. 18 & 20, on the left, were converted from one large house. The deeds of 1666 state that it was situated between the Inn called The Swann (sic) on the one side and the tenement of Wm. Ward, commonly called the Colledge (sic) on the other. The house was bought in 1687 by Samuel Fiske, a charitable gentleman, where he was an apothecary. In 1705, Samuel and John Morley (4) paved the market-place at their own expense. John Baker, a Quaker and former preacher, was largely instrumental in founding the Clayhills Chapel at Pebmarsh. One of the highlights of the early years was a Winkle tea, held every Good Friday, when many people walked from Halstead to join in, armed ready with their pins!

136. The White Hart in 1910

The White Hart dates back to the 15th century, when it consisted of a central hall, with a solar and buttery wing on either side. It is one of the town's oldest coaching inns, being a stage on the London to Gt. Yarmouth service. Note its lovely carved barge boards. St Bartholomew's Day, August 24th 1662, was the last day for the clergy to comply with the requirements of the Act of Uniformity. Two thousand vicars and rectors from all parts of the country refused and were ejected. The Rev. William Sparrow, vicar of St Andrew's church was one of those forced to leave, so he joined together with people sharing his views and the first Non-Conformist church was born, with William as its pastor, in a barn at the rear of the White Hart.

In 1770 constables of Halstead were ordered "to keep the ale-houses in good order and not allow gaming". Social life was increasing and inns were often the venue for functions including feasts, cock-fighting and bull-baiting. As the constables were unpaid they did not go looking for trouble as this was the age of smuggling and highwaymen. In 1759 there were 29 licensed inns in the town including - The Bear, Black Boy, Bell, Cock & Chequers, Cross Keys, Crown, Dolphin, Duke's Head, George, King's Arms, King's Head, Maid's Head, New White Hart, Old Bull, Queen's Head, Rose & Crown, Shoulder of Mutton, Spread Eagle, Star & Garter, Three Horseshoes, Three Pigeons, Two Brewers, Wool Pack and White Horse. Only the Bull, White Hart and Three Pigeons survive today with the same name although some may have new names as it was the proprietor who was issued with the licence and when he moved the sign went along with him. Consequently over the years there could have been several pubs with the same name.

137. Preston Cooper (1877-1950)

Preston Cooper was one of the first drivers of the motor car in Halstead and well-known for his skill and knowledge in anything to do with it. He became acquainted with the mechanism of the internal combustion engine when his brother, Harry, added the repair of motor cars to his cycle manufacture and repair business, installing an inspection pit at 5 Head Street. This resulted in a humorous event - an old gentleman from Maplestead regularly rode into town on his bike, with a box of live chickens tied on the back. One day, not knowing about the alterations, he came down Head Street, steered into Cooper's shop, as he always did and promptly disappeared down the pit, with feathers flying everywhere! Harry and Preston's cycle making business was called the Letches Cycle Works - the name deriving from Letches Farm, the family home. Together they made many "Letches" cycles, including a "triplet" for three riders. One of their cycles built in 1900 for Edmund Frost, was ridden by M.A. Cook, a member of the Brewery firm, to start the 12th Cycle Grand Prix of Essex in March 1965. With the arrival of the motor car, the brothers more or less gave up the cycle making to concentrate on cars and after 1907 transformed the former "Three Crowns" (138) into a garage, which still has motor connections today. With their excellent reputation, they were the only mechanics allowed to service the Rolls Royce of Samuel Courtauld. Harry was used as an emergency service in 1914, when he drove to London in his car at break-neck speed to fetch a surgeon to try to save the life of Mrs Portway after a serious accident (233). The round trip took him five hours. During his early years, Harry was involved in numerous accidents, both cycling and motoring and was thought to lead a charmed life until one fateful day in February 1920 he met his death along the Sudbury road, when a tube burst on his motorcycle. Preston continued with the business in the High Street for the next decade before opening up a General Motor Engineering business with his son Robert, in Bridge Street at the former premises of Harry (Trooper) Goodey. He died in 1950 aged 73 years.

138. 12-23 High Street, c1890

This photo taken before 1890 shows No. 13, now Crossways Garage, next door to the White Hart (136), when the building was the Three Crowns. Although it ceased trading in 1907, the sign lives on in the pargetting. Further down the street at No. 21 was the business of Robert Lake Hughes, a bookseller, stationer and publisher of the East Essex & Halstead Times - a rival of the Halstead Gazette (142). The Times supported the Liberal cause and was established by Robert in 1861, and printed at the rear of the shop. After 32 years the business was sold to Thomas Edmund Clarke, who died less than a year later. Barry & Co continued to publish the paper until its amalgamation with the Gazette in 1921. The shop is now the Card Shop. On the extreme right is the office of Bentall & Robinson, auctioneers & surveyors this business was taken over by Stanley Moger (98) in 1892. Many changes have occurred here and it is currently the Golden Fry. The shop fronts have all changed over the years but the upper floors remain the same.

139. A Friendly Society parade, c1900

Parades like this one were a common sight through the town many years ago. In 1799 the government made trade unions illegal but allowed Friendly Societies, who met in pubs as public halls were few. The coming of the railway made Halstead more accessible, resulting in learned gentlemen coming from London to give lectures on a wide variety of subjects. By 1890 there were about 40 societies including Floral & Horticultural, Amateur Dramatic & Music, Rifle and other Sport's Clubs, Sons of Temperance, the Co-operative Movement, the Foresters, Bricklayers and Oddfellows, also the Working Men's Club. The members of these societies would assemble in Adams' Brewery yard (236) and led by the Town Band paraded up the street as far as the Greenwood School in Head Street (92) then return to St Andrew's Church for a service, collecting money on the way for the Cottage Hospital and other worthy causes.

Before the days of radio and television the Halstead Town Band was in great demand for their music, headed many processions and played at local fetes and social functions. In 1951 they joined the names of the big bands who played background music in films, when they appeared in some scenes of a comedy film, "Nothing to Lose", filmed at Thaxted. In one scene they had to play in the pouring rain which was not enough for the producer who added a fire hose as well.

140. A view of the High Street, c1910

Robert Bourchier, who fought at the Battle of Crecy with the Black Prince, was eager to establish a college or chantry for eight priests in Halstead, but died of the plague in 1349. However, Bartholomew, his grandson was able to grant his wish by arranging the building of the college in 1412, three years after his own death, with the number of priests reduced to five, on an area now occupied by 22-30 High Street. Part of the original structure with a front added in 1731, is still incorporated into No. 26, the former home of Wm. Holman, a local historian. He lived there circa 1700, whilst a master at the nearby Grammar School (144). He writes "it had a large porch jutting out into the street and on the East window plate were the Arms of the Bourchiers carved." In 1770 the premises were occupied by Thomas Neave, a peruke maker - a wig of the type worn by men in the 17th and 18th centuries. During the 1600s the site of 22-24 was described as a "messuage of Wm. Ward, commonly called the college." The large red brick house built on the college site is recorded in "Old and New Halstead " by W.J. Evans, as having been built by James Scarlett, who came to the town from Jamaica and regretted not having it erected further back, with a carriage drive up to it, but an Essex Archaeology Society's report dated 1904 states that the house was built by Samuel Medows, whose coat of arms is displayed in the pediment over the Venetian semi-circular window. This building is one of the finest examples of Georgian architecture and during 1974 won a top conservation award then described as being constructed by a local tradesman in the 18th century. Who is right? During World War I this former home of Mrs Johnson, widow of the pastor of the High Street Congregational Church (152), was offered by the Trustees as a home for Belgian refugees, where they were fed, clothed and given gifts by the locals. The house was commandeered by the military during the following war before No. 24 was converted into three flats for Courtauld employees. The whole building is now the offices of Premaberg. How many remember Mrs Wesolowski, a Polish lady living in one of the flats, who mended nylon stockings after World War II?

141. The day the Circus came to town

Not a common sight in Halstead these days, but during the 1800s and early 1900s the circus was a very popular entertainment. An annual event took place when cages of animals were parked in double rows up the High Street for a week from Barclays Bank to the fountain. For a penny customers could view the animals and for another penny children could ride on an elephant. After a week, everything was moved to Raven's Meadow (191), where the circus took place. Before the 1870s the performance took place on the Market Hill but was stopped due to much obstruction. In 1893, Sanger's Circus came to town with clowns, lady gymnasts, mid-air performers, 295 persons of all nations, 820 horses and ponies, 12 carriages of wild animals, elephants and camels. The photo was probably taken then. The performance was held in a waterproof marquee able to accommodate 20,000 people, preceded by a Grand Procession through the town.

The shop behind the front camels is 26 High Street where Walter William Cooper was a basketmaker, retiring in 1918. His blind father, William, also worked in the same trade in part of the premises that became Banbury & Son, now the florists at the top of the High Street. A little boy was playing in the street with a magnifying glass from a magic lantern in 1921, when No. 26 was a drapery. He was training the sun's rays on to the drawn shop blind, with the result it caught fire. A policeman noticed smoke inside the window but was unable to gain access. The shopkeeper was at church and was summoned to the shop in haste. Realising he had left the key with a relative in church, a window was broken and the fire extinguished. The lad was questioned about the incident, replying, "I played with the glass on the blind when the sun was shining to see if it would set it alight - and it did!" Thanks to the eagle-eyed officer a piece of Halstead's history was saved.

142. The Birthplace of the Halstead Gazette

The repeal of the paper duty enabled many cheap newspapers to be published and the "Halstead & General Advertiser for North Essex", a forerunner of the Halstead Gazette, was the first paper in the county to be sold for the price of one penny (½p). Alfred Carter, of 28 High Street was the founder, who printed the first copy on November 19th 1857, in a large boarded building at the rear of his shop. He had a trial run with the "Halstead Monthly Record" in September of that year, consisting of eight pages recording passing events. His son, Charles, continued with the publication after his father's death in 1883. From its beginning the paper strongly supported the Conservative cause, but obviously not sufficient enough, as some of the party members banded together and bought the copyright in 1887 and had the paper printed by Gurney Benham in Colchester. This proved unsatisfactory, resulting in fresh premises being acquired in Rosemary Lane - the old ropeworks (214). This did not work out either and by 1894 the Gazette again came under the control of Charles Carter, son of the founder and printed at its original premises until 1907, when the copyright was acquired by William H. Root, of the Caxton Works in Trinity Street. In 1921, the Halstead Gazette was incorporated with the East Essex & Halstead Times, a rival paper and continued to be printed at the Caxton Works by a dedicated band of workers until 1966, when it was merged with the Essex County Standard. Carter's shop is now Wardale, Williams and Partners and the house next door is W.H. Brown, estate agents.

143. The White House in the early 1900s

Hidden behind this wisteria covered Georgian façade of the White House stands a much older building erected in 1470. Once owned by Mary Ramsey (145) and bequeathed by her to Christ's Hospital, a school in London. For many years it was the home and surgery of various local surgeons and doctors. Other doctors not so fortunate had to rent rooms in private houses - one was 91 Kings Road, the home of the Carruthers family. During the 1930s and 40s three lady doctors used the front room as a consulting room where following patients could hear all that was being discussed. One doctor residing at the White House was Dr Kerr, a familiar little figure often seen riding an old bike on his rounds to visit his ill patients, with his little white dog trotting along behind.

During 1914 a cow being driven to Braintree market ran away up the passage beside the White House and into the garden of Dr Charles Wink. After climbing over a low wall it crashed through the roof of the skittle alley in the Conservative Club next door. The club steward, Tim Rayner, managed to entice the animal through the building and out into the street where it continued to market - making a good price.

A new group surgery opened on July 1st 1968 was built on land which was partly the old station platform and railway track (21) and took the place of surgeries in large houses in different parts of the town - the White House, Chipping House, Dornhurst, Colchester Road and East Dene, Trinity Street.

144. The old Grammar School

Halstead Grammar School was founded in 1594 by Dame Mary Ramsey (145), to teach forty Halstead and Colne Engaine boys, free of charge, from profits gained from lands of William Martin. The date over the porch in the photo is 1825. In 1861 plans were made to build a new school in Manfield, but these were abandoned, resulting in the High Street premises being enlarged the following year and taking on a new look with the school's initials "HGS" depicted in the gable brickwork. The date 1862 appears over the heavy wooden door on the right side of the building, with the school motto "Get Wisdom, Forget it not". The entrance to the school was through this door and up a flight of stone steps, into a very high, badly lit room, where the boys had to sit from 9.30-12.30 and 2-4.30 without a break. A Scripture lesson of 45 minutes started the day but as there was no timetable for lessons, no one knew what was next. English, French, Latin and Literature took up much of the time, with very little Maths and no Science, Art, Singing or Physical Exercise. One day their thick oak desktops were planed, removing all names that had been etched on them. They were told that for 2/6d (12½p) per letter, a lot of money in those days, they could carve again. The boys did not think much to the idea and promptly hacked their initials in the plaster on the wall just inside the door that leads from the High Street, where they remain today. The Constitutional Club, formed in 1887, first met at the back of 53/55 High street (156), moving to the old ropewalk (214) in 1904. The school closed in 1906 and the building bought by Stanley Moger early in 1910 and opened up as the "Con" Club with 300 members eight months later. The foundation board hanging on the wall was displayed at the Girls' Grammar School for many years, finally being transferred to the Ramsey.

145. Dame Mary Ramsey

Mary Ramsey was the eldest daughter of William Dale, a merchant of Bristol, where she was born. She became the second wife of Sir Thomas Ramsey, a grocer who served as Lord Mayor of London in 1577 and owned much property in Essex. Mary died in 1601 and was buried in the parish church of Christ Church Hospital, built on the foundations of Grey Friars monastery demolished after the dissolution of monasteries in the1530s by order of King Henry VIII. This church was destroyed in the great Fire of London in 1666 along with a tablet prepared in 1596, recording Mary's benefactions. Another tablet was made from records in Stow's Survey and set up in another church built on the site by Sir Christopher Wren. This was sadly destroyed by enemy bombs during World War II. Dame Mary inherited her husband's fortunes and became a very prosperous lady using her wealth to help support many charities for the benefit of poor people.

146. Halstead Grammar School for Boys, 1905

Back Row : J. Hearn, G. Baker, ? Grugeon, S. Banbury, ? Cox, B. Johnson, W. Butcher, E. Brown, R. Hayward, W. Ungless.

2nd Row : ? Robson, R. Lindsell, ? Monson, J.C. Hartle, S. Stockdale, S.R. Nash, H. Sudbury, L. Smith.

3rd Row : C.J. Evans, W. Hughes, R. Rudderham, R. Sudbury (Assistant Master), S. Savery (Headmaster), ? Suckling, R. Grugeon, R. Rogers, E. Pattison.

Front Row : W. Carter, E. Cocksedge, L. Butcher, H.O. Evans, ? Hutley, R. Root, ? Fairbank, ? Fairbank.

147. The High Street about 1910

The two-storey property on the left of what is now The Centre was demolished in 1967, to make way for the shopping precinct. At the time it was Pudney Peirson's ironmongery and builder's merchant, who transferred to a new depot on the Bluebridge Industrial Estate (6). A previous owner was Charles Portway of Tortoise Stove fame (216) and it was here that he handmade the first stove to heat his warehouse in the 1850s. He resided at The Croft, the three-storey house next door, that was partly demolished in 1914 to erect the Halstead branch of the London, County and Westminster Bank. Part of the old house was left intact to serve as a residence for the bank manager. Way back in the 1870s the shop on the extreme right was Ward's, a bootmaker, remaining in that trade until becoming associated with the other end of the body - the hair. The first hairdresser in 1876 was Henry York, then Walter Pawsey, followed by Robert Tatlow who was succeeded by the Co-op, until another trade to do with bodies was introduced - a butcher!

148. Gatehouse Yard, off the High Street

In thc 1880s there were at least seven cottage lined yards tucked away behind the High Street shops, housing nearly 200 people in 50 dwellings. One of these was Gatehouse Yard comprising of twelve old cottages and thought to be an entry to the old vicarage ground or to an area called the Town Garden situated at the rear of the High Street. The deeds of The Croft (147) when owned by Mr Portway mentions the fact that its garden was once part of the Town Garden and is quite near to Gatehouse Yard. The ancient gateway dates from at least the Tudor period and at one time had two massive gates. A few of the cottages are visible in this old photo taken about 1900. It was fashionable at that time for the Council to lay hard-wearing granite blocks across entrances such as Gatehouse Yard and between 57 & 59 High Street. The blocks proved to be very dangerous as leather soles and metal studs (blakeys) could not grip the slippery surface resulting in many falls and broken bones. Today just one cottage remains and the rest have been redeveloped.

149. Gatehouse Yard in the 1960s

A more recent view of Gatehouse Yard taken in the 1960s, shows 45 High Street, the newsagents shop of Fred and Dorothy Brewer on the right. They moved there in 1939, taking over from Alfred Arnold, a fruiterer turned confectioner. The little shop was open seven days a week for the sale of newspapers, periodicals, cigarettes and confectionery. Every Saturday night a crowd gathered outside eagerly awaiting the arrival of the "Green Un" so they could check the football results. On the other side of Gatehouse Yard there were two shops. No. 41 was the hairdressing salon of Sid Sinclair that had previously been "On-the-Square" Library Ltd., the largest lending library in East Anglia, with a large selection of the latest books for all tastes at 2d (1p) per volume for seven days, opening in 1937. At the same time Mr C.H. Nevell opened a high class china shop next door where he traded for 21 years. The two premises were then converted into one shop.

NEVELL
43 HIGH STREET
THE
C
H
I
N
A
SHOP
Phone 230
HALSTEAD

150. The old Post Office, High Street, in the early 1900s

Robert Columbus Hughes, a printer and publisher, was the town's postmaster in 1862, at 40 High Street, now Hume's Bakery. Adjoining, on the left, were old houses and a milliner's shop, later becoming a furniture warehouse. Robert's fifth and youngest son, Henry Lake Hughes worked as a cabinet maker for many years at the warehouse premises but gave up to succeed his father as postmaster in 1872, a position he held for 38 years. Henry decided to pull down that portion of his property on the corner of Chapel Street in 1894 to erect this grand building, which opened the following year. The ground floor was leased by the Post Office authorities, but the upper floors were retained for his residence. The expansion of the Post Office business, especially in the telephone and telegraph departments, demanded more space forcing the Hughes family to give up their apartments and move to a new house in Chapel Street - Westbourne. By 1932 the building was owned by Stanley Moger, who still leased it to the Post Office. A larger sorting room, lorry and cycle sheds were needed, resulting in the demolition of five cottages at the rear in Chapel Street. This is the reason why the house numbers today begin at No. 6. Unfortunately for the tenants they had to find alternative accommodation but probably for the best as the first four cottages had to share two outside loos situated in the front gardens. The Post Office closed in 1964 and moved to new premises next door (154), but the old office still displays memories of the past - the Royal Coat of Arms in the gable end, the words Post Office over the front window and a toehold in the wall in Chapel Street, in which the duty policeman could raise himself up with the aid of a handle, to look through the window to see that all was well inside.

151. Rev. Benjamin Johnson

At the close of a service held on January 2nd 1833, Benjamin Johnson was requested to become the first pastor of the High Street Congregational Church. He accepted, was ordained a few weeks later and laid the foundation stone on May 13th 1833. He died in 1874, having been pastor for 41 years and at his funeral members of all denominations paid tribute to a much respected man. He had been married twice, his second wife Sarah survived him by nearly 40 years. After the church was closed, bodies were exhumed from the vaults beneath to be re-interred at the cemetery in 1949. There were 22 bodies in total, including seven infant children of the Rev. Johnson, who all died before 1854.

152. High Street Congregational Church

The High Street Congregational Church, founded in 1833, was described as having seating accommodation for 600 worshippers. Many of the pews were of the "horse-box type" with upright backs and enclosed by a door. Near the pulpit and at the rear there were square built family seats, some enclosed with curtains. Singing was unaccompanied at first, then later led by an orchestra of wood and stringed instruments. Due to the lack of musicians an organ was eventually purchased. Negotiations were made to join the church with the New Congregational Church in Parsonage Street (201), where united services were held during the years of World War II. This eventually happened in 1946, leaving a redundant building in the High Street, which was bought by the G.P.O. who produced plans for a new Post Office (154). It is interesting to note that the road beside the chapel did not take the name Chapel Street until about 1860. Before then Chapel Street was what we now know as Trinity Street and took its title from the chapel situated in the area where Trinity Church was built.

153. The High Street, c1900

The house to the left of the church was built by Isaac Walford of the Brewery House (158), who made arrangements that on his demise it should become the residence for the minister. He was warned that he would have to make a gift of it during his lifetime but could not be persuaded to do so. The inevitable happened on his death in 1849 and the property was put up for sale by the Court of Chancery. The Rev B. Johnson went to the sale and made a very small bid - the only one made. This was rejected and the Lot was referred back to the Court who offered it to him for £218. He purchased it himself then set about raising the money required and gave instructions that it be conveyed to the Trustees. Friends far and near sent contributions and by 1859 the cost was met and the property became The Manse, belonging to the church. During World War II the cellar was used as an Air Raid shelter and after the church became united with the Congregational Church in 1946, the Manse became derelict and a compulsory purchase order was made. Eventually it came into the possession of the Post Office and demolished in 1959 along with the church to make way for the new Post Office.

154 & 154a.
The High Street in the 1960s

Views taken 60-70 years later of the same area as the previous photo look completely different. The Eastern National Bus garage and office was erected in 1938 on the site once occupied by The Manse, two cottages and the Brewery House and was replaced by Gateway, a supermarket, in 1984. The church was demolished and a new Post Office, built by Pudney & Son Ltd of Colne Engaine - the same firm that erected the one next door (150) in 1895. Arthur E. Evans, chairman of the Halstead District Council, performed the opening on February 12th 1964 and was first in the queue to buy a Savings Certificate for his granddaughter.

As today's postmen nip round the villages in their vans we must spare a thought for those making deliveries before motorised transport. Arthur Hatfield, a Halstead postman in the 1800s, travelled to Chappel everyday leaving mail at Earls Colne and Wakes Colne post offices on the way. For this purpose he had a horse and cart, leaving Halstead at 6am. On reaching his destination he delivered letters etc on foot to the farms and cottages then during the day made boots in a shed not far from the viaduct then returned to Halstead in the early evening. Along the way he blew a whistle to notify people that he was approaching and they could bring out their letters for him to bring back to Halstead to be sent on their way.

155. The High Street, 1892

This crowd was gathered outside what is now Somerfields supermarket, during the Election campaign of 1892, when the successful Charles W. Gray, of Stanstead Hall, stood against C.J.S. Dodd. Annually this area was a hive of activity as the large gates, on the left, led to H. Brown's tanyard (43). People were attracted to the many waggons and carts loaded with bark, lining the street, waiting their turn to unload in the tannery yard. Stripped from oak trees, the bark used for tanning leather, was stacked in the dry and transported from as far away as Chelmsford and Cambridge. Extra workers were employed to bring in the 800-900 tons.

Tanning is one of the trades that has disappeared from the town along with - woolstapler, bay & say maker, fellmonger, silk manufacturer, basket maker, tallow chandler, cooper, breeches maker, glover, gunsmith, miller, strawplaiter, pawnbroker, cheesemonger, broom maker, papermaker, rope-maker, town crier, brick & tile maker, tinsmith, taxidermist, wireworker, walking stick and umbrella maker, pelisse (fur cloak) maker and peruke (wig) maker.

156. Percy Walls, boot & shoemaker, c1925

Way back in the 1800s, 53 High Street was a carriageway for horses and carts to reach a blacksmith's at the rear, with a room over the top belonging to No. 55. By 1890, part of the access was transformed into a shop window leaving a narrow passage on the left for access to the back yard, from where stairs led to a long hall, stretching from the back of No. 55, over a kitchen and two or three workshops. This hall is where the Conservative Club was formed, being large enough to support two full size billiard tables. This and two upper rooms fronting the High Street over the shoe shop and passage were hired from Nathaniel Robinson, a bootmaker and steward of the club. In 1898, the carriageway was converted into two small rooms behind the showcase window and at right angles to the street, leaving a narrow passageway on the left for access. The first room became the County Court and the other was a small dairy. Standing in the doorway of his shop is Percy Walls who made gentlemen's handsewn riding boots at Joseph Tiffen's workshop at 3 Head Street. After losing his job for taking time off after his wedding, Percy started his own business in Highbury Terrace. A short time later he moved to a little shop beside the Swan (160), a former butcher's, before transferring to No. 55 in 1913. As he was unfit for Military service in World War I, he was given the job of repairing the boots of 1,000 soldiers camped at Ashford Lodge, Sudbury Road, representing a lot of footwear. As his workshop was not big enough to cope and all horses had been commandeered by the Army, a large soldier volunteered to pull a cart loaded with mending gear to the camp, where Percy and his staff worked under the trees. In 1931 Henry Walker, an outfitter, was given notice to leave his shop at 66 High Street and had nowhere to go, so Percy gave up the shop window at No. 53 to allow Henry to move into the former County Court, with the front window in which to display his goods. The shop still trades under the name of Walker and No. 55 is still in the shoe trade but no longer handmade.

157. 57 High Street in 1935

Albert Chaplin and Dick Keeble worked together at the Atlas Works, Earls Colne, before Albert left to take over the cycle engineering business of John Smyth. Within a few months Dick followed and joined his friend as a partner. They gave cycle tuition and built their "Go-Easy" cycles on the premises. In 1960 Albert Chaplin, the founder's son carried on the trade, extending it to include a department for mopeds and motor cycles in the charge of George Bowman. The decorations on the shop front were for the Silver Jubilee celebrations for King George V in 1935. Red, white and blue crepe paper was used, then much to everyone's dismay, rain on the morning ruined the display. Young Win Chaplin had to run up the street to Banbury's to buy some muslin in the appropriate colours, then quickly make some bunting to replace the soggy paper - the result can be seen in the photo. Before the formation of the cycle business, the shop was for many years a bakery. My Gt Gt Grandfather Robert Payne was a baker there in the mid 1800s where he sold bread, confectionery, ginger beer (homemade), life assurance and newspapers - quite an assortment. During this same period there were no fewer than 22 bakers dotted around the town making the daily bread.

158. A sleepy High Street, pre 1895

Unlike the rest of the High Street, the lower end has had many changes on the left, as you can see from this view taken c1893. The foliage covered house, the home of the tanyard manager, was said to have been 500-600 years old in 1909, and the oldest residence in the town that had never been rebuilt since its original construction. It was demolished in 1937/8 to make way for the Eastern National Omnibus Company's office and garage (154). The area between the Brewery House, part of which is Bairstow Eves, and Chapel Street has all been redeveloped, including the two-storied warehouse that was removed for the building of the old Post Office (150) on the corner of Chapel Street.

To the right of the horse and cart stands a shop that was Fleet's for many years and is now Options. In the early part of the 20th century J.A. Bird ran the shop before his son-in-law Arthur Buck took over. Mr Bird was a fruiterer, fishmonger, poulterer and ice merchant. Large blocks of ice were delivered by lorry from the Colchester Ice Company and stored in a zinc lined cold store at the back of the premises where he also had a Smoke House. It was here, over burning oak logs, that he suspended fresh herrings, transported from the coast by rail, to produce home-cured bloaters that sold for 4d (2p) per pound.

159. The High Street before the age of the motor-car

No, not a one-horse town, but Halstead during the turn of the 20th century, looking quite different from today and with no need for a pedestrian crossing. There has been a complete change on the left-hand side up to Chapel Street, even the Royal Oak has changed its appearance. The International Stores next to the pub, started trading in 1890 as the International Tea Company Stores. During the early 1900s the business was temporarily based at 26 High Street whilst rebuilding took place, returning to the original site until its closure on November 15th 1975. Curry's then transferred from smaller premises, now part of the present Lloyd's/TSB, into the shop which today is Clinton Cards. The area was connected to transport of one form or another for many years - horses, coaches, cars then a boot & shoe shop belonging to P.C. Hayward from whom F.W. Woolworth acquired it in 1934 and is still trading today.

Opposite, after trading for 36 years, J & J Symonds, 63/65 High Street, were forced to close their grocery shop in 1918 after the local Food Committee considered it to be unnecessary. Herbert Richardson a baker of 32 Head Street then purchased the premises for his bakery where he made exceedingly good cakes, bread and chocolates, winning many prizes and diplomas for his goods. After his death at a young age his wife and son continued the business. One member of staff won a local beauty contest and had to live with the name of Donut Queen. The shop is now Premier Travel who bought the shop from Tooks bakers.

160. High Street, c1896

Still in the age of the horse, the condition of the street was somewhat appalling. In 1857, a Halstead man was fined 29/-, including costs, for obstructing the Road Surveyor, who was placing pieces of wood round a worn part of the High Street "in order that the sides of the road would have equal share of the traffic". Imagine that happening with today's traffic! On the right is The Swan, a pub previously called The Ship. The landlord, at the time the photo was taken, Henry Neave, also ran the butcher's shop situated on the left side of the pub, where carcasses can be seen hanging outside. The Swan was demolished to be replaced by Lipton's Self-Service Store, opening July 2nd 1963, later taken over by Boots the Chemist.

With so many horses being used for transport, the roads were very messy. This forced the powers that be to engage a lad with a wheelbarrow and broom "to keep the road clear of horse droppings and rubbish" from the Cedars, Sudbury Road to the Prince of Wales' Oak (31) for the princely sum of five shillings (25p) a week. He must have had the day off when this photo was taken!

161. Lower High Street, c1946

This photo was taken just after World War II when the Trustees Savings Bank opened a small branch at 68 High Street, to the right of Oak Yard. Next door was Curry's into which the bank extended when the latter moved to larger premises at the former International Stores (159). The two small shops to the left of the Royal Oak were demolished in 1949 and Mence Smith's, hardware shop erected on the site - later becoming John Winter Drake's, jewellers, in 1966. Now we come to the Royal Oak, formerly one of the town's principal posting houses, where horse drawn coaches stopped to set down and pick up passengers. Before being a public house it was two cottages with gardens in front, where an apricot tree and grapevine grew against the walls. The area has seen much rebuilding over the years. A suggestion was made in 1910 for the "amusement and instruction" of young men of the town in Winter evenings. This resulted in an Amateur Boxing Club commencing on October 28th of that year, behind the Oak with twenty members.

162. The entrance to Factory Lane East, c1920

How many people remember the Hardware shop of Henry Pountney on the left of the entrance to 'Factory Lane' and Charlie Parsonson's shop on the right? Charlie was a basketmaker for over 60 years and some of his wares can be seen hanging outside. The shop was part of Adelaide House, a milliner's during the mid 1800s, trading under the name of M.A. Reeve. At that time crinolines were fashionable and were sold from 2/9d (14p) each, with a choice of bonnets and hats and a service where they could be cleaned, dyed and altered.

A Poem written in the 1920s about the High Street

As you walk down High Street, Halstead,
And look at the windows gay,
You feel as you gaze at Richardson's (159)
You are thousands of miles away.

Next Peirson's (147) takes your fancy,
And you picture yourself at home,
With that dainty companion and fender,
A nice fire and no wish to roam.

As you sit by this cosy fireside,
With your feet near the fender bright,
Some fruits from Bird's (158) lovely assortment,
Would finish the picture alright.

Then when the smouldering embers
Tell you that bed-time is near,
No cold neath that feathery eiderdown
From Clark's (130) - you ever need fear.

Then when the cold winds of winter
Make the snowflakes around you float,
Right gladly you go to Simmons' (15)
For a cosy, comfy coat.

With all these good things around you,
You're not always up to par;
So you visit Wright the chemist (133)
For physic and Wright's coal tar.

Just a word of consolation
To the rest of the shops in the town;
For they really deserve great credit,
And their goods are of high renown.

There's no need to travel to Colchester,
Though buses run to and fro;
For food and clothing in Halstead
Is as cheap in the long run you know.

If you wish your business to prosper,
In Summer as well as in Winter;
You'll be really wise if you advertise
With Root (142) - the well-known printer.

163. The lower High Street in the late 1800s

This row of ancient little buildings stood at the bottom of the High Street until 1904, when they were purchased by the Co-op who demolished the middle three - Culyer's newsagents, a cottage and T. Miller's fishmongers - to make way for the Drapery & Hardware Departments erected on the site (164). The shop on the left sold clothes until 1915 when the Home & Colonial Ltd grocery took over the lease, which terminated in the early 1950s when it was taken over by the Halstead Co-operative Society Ltd and moved to the corner of Trinity Square, now Paynie's (232).

163a Co-op Delivery van of the era

164. The lower part of the High Street in the 1950s

Here we see the same area as in the previous photo but taken in the 1950s, after the termination of the Home & Colonial lease and the purchase of the basketmaker's shop (162), enabling the Co-op to make many alterations. The whole back of this site was built over to make a large furnishing showroom, with a front entrance through the shop on the corner of Factory Lane East. At the same time Sharpley's, adjoining the Co-op drapery was purchased and turned into the Hardware shop. Other improvements have taken place over the years. In the early 1970s the Halstead Industrial Co-operative Society Ltd was taken over by the Ipswich Co-operative Society Ltd and is now the Co-operative Society (Ipswich & Norwich) Ltd.

TELEPHONE NO.: HALSTEAD 6
SUDBURY 79
HEDINGHAM 12

ALL COMMUNICATIONS TO BE ADDRESSED TO THE SOCIETY
AND NOT TO INDIVIDUALS

TELEGRAMS:
CO-OPERATIVE SOCIETY
HALSTEAD, EX.

HALSTEAD
INDUSTRIAL CO-OPERATIVE SOCIETY LIMITED.

REGISTERED OFFICE:
Trinity Street
HALSTEAD
ESSEX

BRANCH STORES
NORTH ST., SUDBURY, SUFFOLK
SWAN ST., SIBLE HEDINGHAM
COAL WHARF
FACTORY LANE, HALSTEAD
& STATION ROAD, SUDBURY

GROCERY, BAKERY
BOOT & SHOE
BOOT REPAIRING
OUTFITTING
DAIRY
} TRINITY ST., HALSTEAD

DRAPERY
BUTCHERY
FURNISHING
} HIGH ST., HALSTEAD

REFERENCE TO YOUR LETTER

IN YOUR REPLY REFER TO
P 36 ES/DS

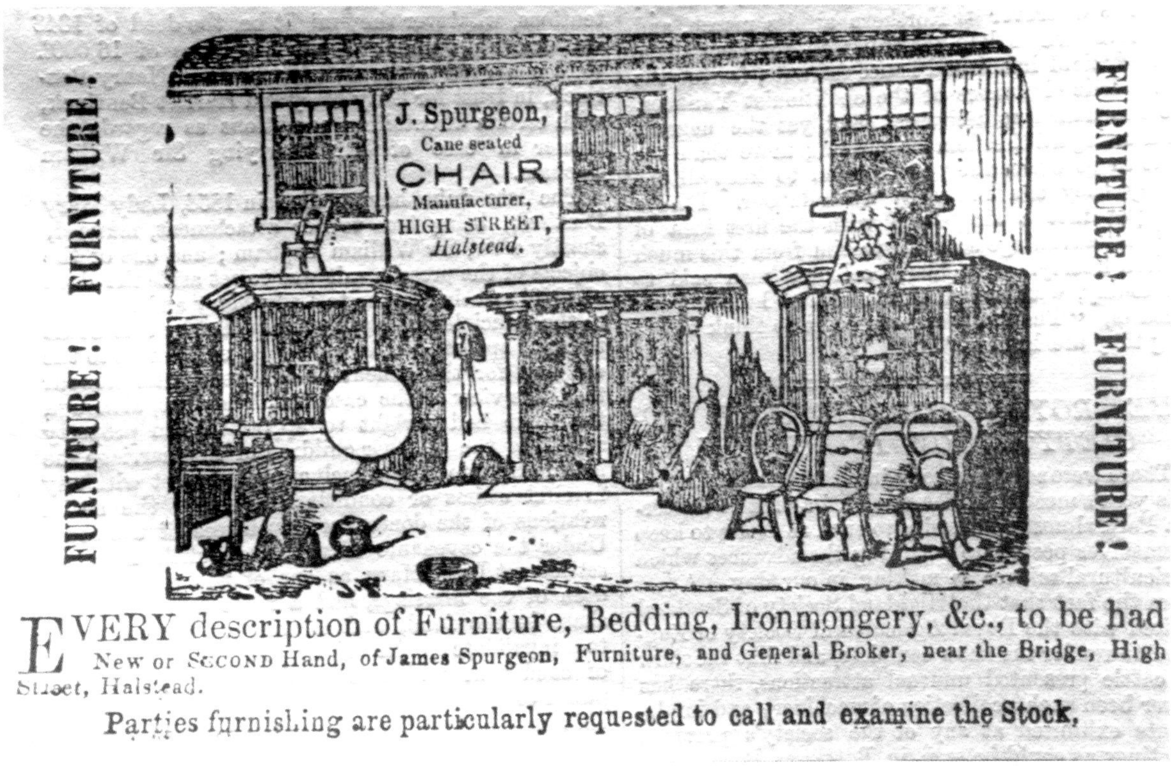

165. An advertisement of 1862

An 1862 advert of James Spurgeon depicts his shop at the bottom of the street, now a restaurant and charity shop. In 1896 the business was purchased by Nathan William Pendle, who continued to make furniture, including Essex chairs, on the premises. His son Herbert joined him in 1906 and his two daughters ran a china and hardware department. Furniture was delivered by horse and cart from the shop which remained open until 10pm on Saturdays. The family traded here for 67 years and many local people still refer to the area as Pendle's corner.

The Guild of the Holy Trinity

Guilds were ancient brotherhoods in England before the Norman Conquest, beginning as small burial and benefit societies. The word Geld or Yeld meant yield and signified "a payment, offering or tribute". It was an association of people contributing money for the mutual aid and protection for members in a particular trade or craft, in which they were engaged. There was always a strong religious element and the richer guilds maintained a chaplain of their own and a chantry chapel. Their meetings were called "guild-ales" and in many towns replaced the older authority, developed into the governing body of the town and their guildhall became the Town Hall. Recorded in a Deed dated 1527, Halstead's guildhall (166) had a Farrye Clerk (Chantry priest) belonging to it and the Guild of the Holy Trinity played an important part in government and order of the town, combining in itself the functions of a Chamber of Commerce, Friendly Society, Board of Guardians, Urban District Council and Ratepayer's Association. Their chapel was situated near Trinity Church (33).

166. The old Guildhall, c1899

There was a great controversy in the 1970s over the preservation of Jack Root's butcher's shop (169), thought by conservationists to be the old Guildhall, and ought to be saved. It was realised too late that the Guildhall was in fact the adjoining structure, facing up the street that had already been demolished and Martin's, the newsagents, built on the site. A report in the Gazette in 1898 states that the building at the bottom of the High Street, occupied by Robert Nash, butcher, had been extensively renovated and was a very old house, probably one of the oldest in the town. The deeds revealed that it was the old guildhall and dated back to the 15th century and was the first property purchased by John Morley (4)for £50, selling it within four months at great profit - a start that was to make him a fortune in landjobbing. How sad that this part of Halstead's history was allowed to be lost when this information was available.

167. A slaughterhouse of the 1800s

This gruesome photo was taken circa 1870 at the slaughterhouse of Gabriel D. Green. Edward Amey is wielding the pole-axe with Gabriel at the head of the animal and Dakin Green, his son at the rear. Edward worked as a butcher for the Green family practically all his life, until the business was taken over by Robert Nash. The shop and slaughterhouse was part of the old Guildhall (166). The meat trade was flourishing in the town during the 19th century and in November 1893 no fewer than 12 slaughterhouses are recorded - six belonged to retail butchers, six to pork butchers and dealers who slaughtered solely for London. Another meat connection was the bullock skins that were brought to Halstead on the train and delivered to the Tan yard (43) to be made into leather. Many skins still had flesh attached to the rump end and hard up workers would slice the meat off to take home to feed hungry mouths. This meat was referred to as "Rumpsheba". If the flesh was maggot infested the local fishermen collected it for bait - nothing was wasted.

168. The lower High Street, c1906

Changes have been made here since this photo was taken of young people posing in the road. William Barker's grocery shop, on the left of the bridge was demolished in 1911 for the widening of the latter. One little shop that has hardly changed is No. 99, which has for many years been associated with either fruit, vegetables or flowers. During World War I the shop, run by Mr H. North, was a collection point for fruit stones and nutshells to be made into charcoal to put into anti-gas masks. In 1921 George Lock, a well-known figure in the Horticultural world, took over the business with this wife. He was a Fellow of the Royal Horticultural Society and honorary life member of the British Gladiolus Society for 30 years service. He was the Society's honorary test garden superintendent and in his nursery gardens at Chapel Street, behind the White House (143), now Elizabeth Way he had the Society's trial ground. He grew his own produce to sell in the shop and seeds were kept in little wooden drawers ready to be weighed out by the ounce for a few pence. George was also a judge at the Chelsea Flower Show in 1959.

169. Another butcher's shop near the river, c1897

Here we see Fred Fletcher (right), in the doorway of his shop near the bridge. He was associated with the business for over 50 years and was in charge of the sausagemaking department for 17 years before taking over the ownership from Mrs M. Spurgeon, a pork butcher and sausage maker in September 1897. He also held a licence to sell beer until 1907. Morton, his son, succeeded him until 1929 when Jack Root bought the business. A mistake was made in 1973 when planners thinking the shop was the old Guildhall, preserved it by making a walkway through after the real building had been demolished. By the river side of the shop before 1887, a Mr Prentice hired out boats for 4d (2p) and trips were taken up the river as far as Box Mill where at the time there was a wooden windmill.

170. Decorations for the Coronation, 1953

Now an entrance to the Solar but at the time of the photo, it led to Courtauld's factory (78) and was decorated for the coronation of Queen Elizabeth II. At one time this area was called "Old Tan Yard" as it led to an early tannery, established as long ago as 1570. At its entrance stood two massive gates through which a meadow was entered - now the site of Solar. In this meadow John Greenwood treated 700 poor people to a dinner when Peace was proclaimed after the Battle of Waterloo in 1815. Before the 20th century many yards were situated behind the High Street shops and "Old Tan Yard" appears to have been the largest. In 1881 it consisted of 16 dwellings, one of which was empty. In the remaining lived a total of 47 adults and 27 children.

171. The Iron footbridge in 1920

If you stand at the Kings Road/Factory Lane West junction today you will see a completely different scene. When the railway (208) came, it cut the town in two, resulting in the need for a footbridge to replace a former footpath. First a wooden structure (210) was erected to span the station yard in 1860, but by the end of that year complaints were being made that it was slippery, dangerous and wearing away. After many years of repairs and serious arguments this longer replacement iron bridge was constructed, probably about 1904, when the yard was extended. Not only was it a shortcut for many workers but a vantage point for trainspotting and watching the activity on the lines. It was also a platform from where children would try to toss coins etc, into the funnels of steam trains as they passed underneath, many going home covered in smuts from the smoke. This photo was captured by Arthur Nice in 1920, with his "five bob box camera" from behind a decorative iron fence made at Portway's foundry. Sadly most of the town's garden ironwork was requisitioned during World War II, with just a few gates remaining and a fence still stands round the Mill House in Mill Chase. The footbridge lasted until November 1965, becoming a victim of acetylene cutters after the closure of the railway.

172. Nos. 69-73 Kings Road, c1920

Before the Colne Valley Railway came in 1860 this road did not exist but later a roadway named New Road was taken through to Trinity Street, running parallel to the railway. A change of name to Railway Road occurred before finally being called Kings Road in 1890. In the early years a builder, John King, then lived at No. 1, from whom the road took its name. He was the son of John, also a builder, who erected a large number of old business premises in the town. Another John King, his grandfather, was pastor of Hedingham Road Baptist Church (101), then North Street, from 1808-1832. These three houses in Kings Road were purchased by the Essex County Council about 1920, for police accommodation, in a terrace then known as One Pot Row. Did the name stem from the fact that each house had one chimney pot? For many years an Essex Constabulary badge was displayed over the front doors of these properties.

173. A mechanical elephant, c1950

At the Parsonage Street end of Kings Road stands Hunwicks, on a piece of land which, in 1901, was laid out with a track for the Halstead Cycle Club. The land was later acquired by the Halstead Co-operative Society, who duly sold it to Mr Harrison, facilitating the setting up of W.A. Hunwicks steel fabricating business in 1949, from the old Paper Mill (41). Why a photo of an elephant you may ask? The answer - Frank Stuart of Thaxted, designed mechanical elephants for which Hunwicks made the frames and workings, circa 1950. The frames were delivered to Mr Stuart, a theatrical mask maker, who covered them with specially treated ½ inch thick paper. The elephant was driven by a man sitting astride the neck with up to ten children on its back. It was powered by an 8 h.p. engine, giving a walking speed of 2-12 miles per hour, with an exhaust pipe coming down the trunk. The ears flapped as the head swayed from side to side. Thirty thousand parts went into this 8ft 6in tall animal and it is said that one was used in Eisenhower's election campaign in America. Apparently in 1952 Mr Stuart had a disagreement with his backers and went bankrupt as a result. Hunwicks claim to be able to make anything "From a pin to an elephant!".

174. Feoffee's Barn in the 1890s

Feoffee's Barn originally stood in the corner of Barn Pasture until a road was made to run in front of it in 1862. Another 28 years passed before this road joining Railway Road (Kings Road) and New Street was named Martins Road. The barn, property of Martin's Charity, was used to store crops deposited as a rent and the proceeds were used for many years to annually distribute about 800 shirts and shifts to poor people. William Martin was a great benefactor, with extensive properties in the town and district. He was a wealthy clothier and died in 1573, leaving a remarkably detailed Will, giving details of his wide ranging possessions.

In 1875, one young lad watched four men using flails, threshing the corn in the barn at the time when horse-drawn reapers were cutting the corn in Man Field - now Pretoria and Morley Roads. This boy grew up to be the well-known artist and local headmaster, Morton Mathews. The barn was demolished sometime in the 1890s. This photo of the barn is, as far as I know, the only one in existence but there are a few paintings. The gentleman on the extreme left is Charlie Bragg, who ran a little corner shop on the Hedingham Road/Upper Chapel Street junction (100) and sold winkles from a pony and cart.

175. North Mills, known locally as Frost's Mill, c1900

Originally a post mill stood on this site in Mill Chase, off Hedingham Road, way back in the 1720s, before being replaced by a Smock Mill 70 years later which was retowered in 1820. In 1827 "materials for building a post mill" belonging to Joseph Greenwood, once a partner of Thomas Frost, were auctioned and at the time it was stated that "the whole having been rebuilt within the last 7 years". It was then that eight discarded elm curb segments from a mill were built into a house in the town, as lintels over the windows. In November 1867, the mill was tail-winded causing the cap and sails to crash into the yard. After this disaster the windmill was repaired and a steam mill erected behind it in 1868, enabling the sails to be driven either by wind or steam power. The mill house (right) was formerly two cottages of low design with flattish roofs, allowing the wind to pass over. A third storey was added to the steam mill in 1897 with the aid of scaffolding erected within inches of the path of the sails. A builder failed to heed a warning about the danger of the sails should the wind change direction and was scooped off the staging and dropped into the yard below, sustaining injuries that left him deformed. Windpower was abandoned in 1907 and the cap and sails were removed in 1922. Further deterioration forced the removal of the wooden smock framing in 1947, leaving the brick base, which survives today. A mill, then called Boisfield Mill, was taken over by Thomas Frost starting off a business in 1720 that ended with Alan Frost and his son Gretton being last in a long line, running the family firm, which ceased trading in 1989. The steam mill was converted into luxury housing but the mill area and house still remain in the family.

176. Lucy Greenwood (1825-1895)

Lucy was born in 1825, one of eight children of Joseph & Elizabeth Greenwood, a local Quaker family. She wanted to devote her life to the welfare of the poor and friendless, intending to take them in to educate and train. Lucy found some waifs and strays in the local area, the first two were orphans whose parents had died from smallpox. Whilst in London she came across many more and brought them back to Halstead in their rags. With the help of Friends of the Quaker faith she was able to devote her time, talents and love, invaluable to more than 400 girls passing through her hands and out into the world much better for it. The 1841 Census records that Lucy was living at Langley Mill, it was here that she jumped into the water near the floodgates to save a child's life, with the result that she went deaf. This deafness gave her a special interest in the deaf and dumb, consequently teaching all her girls the sign language. She retired in 1882 and moved into The Chase (89), where girls who had served their time at the Greenwood School and were unable to get employment, were trained to go into service.

177. The Greenwood School in the 1890s

A school for destitute girls was founded in 1866 by Lucy Greenwood in an old building in Bois Field, now Mill Chase, where she had previously nursed smallpox victims. Halstead Industrial School was its original title, later renamed The Greenwood School in honour of the founder. As the number of girls grew so did the premises. At one end stood Lucy's house, whilst at the other end, overlooking Head Street (92) was a large industrial room, formerly used as the National School. In between, there was a hotch-potch of little half-timbered cottages that were gradually opened out into each other forming a chain all linked together. In the middle, surrounded on three sides stood the Particular Baptist chapel. The original school building, with its long low rooms with broad windows gave good light for the handloom weavers, as it was originally a Bay & Say factory. About 1733 a workhouse was established here and was described as having 17 rooms as well as a brewhouse and hoghouse. A map of 1831 shows this as standing end-on to the road , then called Workhouse Lane and was recalled by Alice Porter who was born in 1832. Later a purpose built workhouse for 400 inmates was erected in Hedingham Road (111). Alice also remembered part of the Greenwood School as the Church Charity Schools, forerunner of St Andrew's School. She also witnessed the laying of Greenstead Green Church foundation stone and remembered all the children returning to town in a double file delighted with the bread and large piece of cheese each had been given. Incidentally she left school at the age of eight years and died in 1927 aged 95 years. Her husband was employed at Courtauld's for 68 years - quite a feat!

The Greenwood School closed in the 1990s and has recently been converted into residential units.

178. Nos. 1-39 Mitchell Avenue in 1900

The Halstead Industrial Co-operative Society Ltd started in June 1860 and was supported in its early days by several well-known families including the Vaizeys and Courtaulds. As it flourished in the late 1800s much land was purchased to develop small housing projects. The land on which these 20 houses stand was once a garden and was bought with fields at the rear and a football field, now King George V playing field in Kings Road. The Society also bought more land in 1895 that belonged to Martin's Charity near Feoffee's Barn (174). The following year five houses in the continuation of New Street needed to be numbered resulting in the road being named Neale Road with Mitchell Avenue adjoining it. These names commemorate two pioneers of the Co-op movement - J.T.W. Mitchell, who started the national movement and E.V. Neale, the General Secretary, a devout man who wrote several hymns. The rent for these Co-op houses in Mitchell Avenue in 1900 was 5/2d (26p) per week for ones with a side door and those without were 5/- (25p).

179. Halstead Fire Brigade, 1957

E.T. Adams and his brother Percy were instrumental in forming the old Halstead Volunteer Fire Brigade in 1878, with other influential men of the town. The first engine was pumped by hand and kept in a building called the Engine House in the garden of Mill House in the Causeway. It was drawn by two horses provided by the Brewery (236). The engine carried a driver plus five firemen to the fire with the remaining men following in a pony and trap. The Council took over the brigade in 1921, after which everything moved to Head Street (94). In 1925 the H.U.D.C. bought a towable Merryweather fire engine and reached an agreement with Mr J.S. Norton, builder, to tow the fire engine behind his lorry when required. This was not a very good arrangement, for often when the alarm was raised, the driver Basil Runtle, was out of town with the lorry. Frantic efforts would be made to locate him then he had to race back to town to pick up the gear, hitch up the fire engine and proceed to the fire, sometimes 45 minutes had passed. Later the engine, a converted lorry, was kept in a shed in Morley Road. In 1957, when the siren sounded a gleaming red and silver engine sped out to hopefully extinguish the flames. These firemen had said 'farewell' to the old engine and lined up beside the new one, specially designed for use in rural areas. In 1968 the station transferred to a purpose built one in Parsonage Street. The firemen are, left to right: Arthur Frost, ?, Ron Britton, Keith Hunt, Jack Seager, Bill Petty, George Finch, Maurice Norman, George Hardy, Dudley Bacon, Jack Crouch, Lloyd Cutting, Frank Felton, Dennis Sibley, Dick Finch, Charles Cracknell and Hazel Bragg.

180. Mount Hill near the "Three Pigeons", c1965

Mount Hill before the mid 1960s was lined with more little cottages than today. Those to the right of the Three Pigeons were demolished to make the new part of Ramsey Road and the entrance into the housing estate that was built off Ramsey Road starting in the late 1960s. The building on the left of the pub was removed to make a car park, along with an oasthouse at the rear, where hops grown in nearby fields were processed over a century ago.

Halstead had a vast water supply with wells and springs everywhere, as some of the old yard names suggest - Well, Spring and Pump. One piped spring stood beside Mount Hill but in 1906 the water became suspect when cases of typhoid fever were reported by people drinking it. The sewer from the Isolation Hospital (181), where there was a case of the fever at the time, passed near the spring. It was decided to relocate and three sites were suggested, 1) higher up the hill on the same side, 2) near the Prince of Wales' Oak (31) and 3) in the bank on the opposite side of the road. The latter won the vote resulting in the drinking fountain being moved in 1908 where it remains today.

181. The Isolation Hospital, c1900

This was Halstead's Isolation Hospital situated "in a most healthy part of town", off Mount Hill. A proposal for the hospital was made in 1894, receiving ten tenders ranging from £1,484 to £1,940 - the former of Harcourt Runnacles was accepted. The hospital, completed in 1896, consisted of three groups of buildings in the Queen Anne style. There were two wards, seen on the right, a nurses cottage (left) and a mortuary. There were two approaches, one from Trinity Road and the other from Mount Hill through an ornamental gateway beside the garage. In July 1938 there was a serious outbreak of poliomyelitis, when 92 cases from Halstead and the neighbouring area were admitted. This hit the headlines in the National Press and took on rather frightening proportions when a press photographer took a photo of a string of Grammar School girls on their way to catch the train home to local villages along the line, as they did every school day. In the papers the next day this was attributed to "a mass evacuation from a town stricken by fear". The hospital was used for the treatment of tuberculous women, for two years from January 1944, then closed due to staffing difficulties. For a short time the premises then served as a Nursery Home where 16 children were cared for by a nurse and four students. In May 1948 the buildings became redundant under the N.H.S. Act and were taken over as the Rural District Council offices from 1951 to March 1974, later becoming a small industrial complex. The site was demolished, cleared and the small housing estate of Clover's built on the land.

182. The Hole, Mount Pleasant, early 1900s

In 1794 a 'Pest House' was referred to as being "on a hill called Paddy Crow". This is the area through which the footpath passes from Coggeshall Pieces to the top of Colne Hill - the old name being Paddock Row. About a hundred years later the local Board of Health turned down a suggestion to convert the cottages at Does Corner (123) for an isolation hospital, in favour of The Hole. This was situated above Mount Pleasant and consisted of two lath and plaster cottages, without drainage of any kind. The rooms were small with very low ceilings and hardly any ventilation. In 1889 it was considered large enough to take eight patients but only as a temporary arrangement as it would not be able to cope should an epidemic occur. If such an emergency had arisen a bell tent was to have been used. The patients were looked after by a kind old lady of considerable experience but no training, who managed well considering her lack of knowledge and medical appliances. The disinfector was a dilapidated horsedrawn four-wheeler cab minus the wheels, in which contaminated clothes were hung and fumigated with sulphur. Also there was no way to isolate different infectious diseases. It served its purpose until 1896 when the new hospital was built (181). Its name originated from the fact that it stood in a saucer shaped site. The cottages were converted into one house which was demolished when the land around De Vere Road was developed in the 1960s.

183. Charrington's shop in the early 1900s

Standing on the corner at the junction of Trinity Road and Mount Pleasant was a flourishing business built up by Edward William Allen, selling grocery, drapery, footwear, hardware, lamp oil and house furnishings - what might be classed as a general store. As well as the shop he had horsedrawn vehicles to travel round the town and villages selling his wares. He acquired the business off Abraham Newton, circa 1892, after working as a traveller for H.C. Knight on the Market Hill until that business went bankrupt. After Mr Allen moved to Clacton, William Charrington bought the business at the end of World War I, which was run as a family concern for many years. The photo was taken outside the shop after the Charringtons had progressed to motorised transport.

184. Cottages in Mount Pleasant now demolished

Halstead was a flourishing town in 1860, with the Colne Valley Railway passing through and hundreds of people being employed at Courtauld's silk factory. Earlier attempts had been made to start a Co-operative Society without success. Eventually the established Rochdale Society was written to for a copy of their rules. A meeting was called on March 3rd 1860 to discuss them, resulting in 29 members each paying 1/- (5p) to join. The seed was sown and the Halstead Society was born. A committee was chosen and a room rented at 29 Mount Pleasant, the house with the white door, which became the first Co-op shop, although trading in a small way. Only flour and sugar were sold at first when the shop was only open in the evenings, with committee members serving voluntarily. All these cottages and others in the road were demolished to make way for the Council development, Cutting Drive. A passageway on the left side of No. 29 led through to Summers Row, a terrace of eight dwellings, also pulled down in the early 1970s. Summers Row was one of the developments built by Wm. Cook (103). He is said to have loved the pleasant things in life and this is reflected in the names of some of his houses - Belle Vue, Garden Terrace and Summers Row.

185. The former Carpenter's Arms

The Carpenter's Arms, one of three public houses situated at the lower end of Mount Pleasant, began its life as a beerhouse one of a group of three cottages. The cottages on the left of the pub were demolished to make way for a car park some years ago, but in 2000 when the redundant pub was converted into two houses, the site was again occupied by two houses.

The Carpenter's Arms featured in the celebration on January 1st 1909 of Old Age Pension Day. The day commenced with the firing of cannons at different local houses and continued at intervals throughout the day. The Town Crier walked the streets announcing that thanks to the Liberal Party, the great boon of pensions for deserving old age had been accomplished. In the evening a large crowd assembled outside the party's headquarters where a torchlight procession started round the town. Led by the Town Band, 60 torchbearers and a score of lads carrying Chinese lanterns suspended from broomsticks and others displaying banners to welcome the old age pension, paraded down the High Street, up Trinity Street and along Trinity Road. On reaching the Carpenter's Arms a halt was made and the band played a selection of music. The parade set off again via New Street, Neale Road, Mitchell Avenue and Kings Road, to the bottom of Tidings Hill where another stop was made before continuing up Parsonage Street to the fountain on the Market Hill where much cheering took place. The parade then returned to the Liberal Club where speeches were made.

186. Bob Curry and his wife Dorothy in the Nag's Head

Within close proximity of one another were, at one time, three public houses trading at the bottom of Mount Pleasant. The Carpenter's Arms (185), the Red Lion, still trading and standing on the site of an earlier pub called the Victoria, which before 1848 went under the sign of the Plough & Sail, no doubt the sail of a windmill. A pub called The Castle was replaced by the Nag's Head in 1938, and has since been converted into residential units. One of the landlords was Robert Curry, known as Bob, a well-known footballer. He was born in Gateshead and on leaving school joined Sheffield Wednesday, making his debut for the Owls in 1937 against Tottenham Hotspur. He was one of the first to be called up at the start of the War and during the hostilities played for his unit until he was 'blown up' at Dunkirk and medically discharged with his injuries and shell shock that kept him out of football for two years. After playing for a short while for Gainsborough Trinity, he joined Colchester United in 1946 where he was appointed team captain and led the 'U's' to the fifth round of the F.A. Cup in 1947/8 before they were defeated by a Blackpool team including the legendary Stanley Matthews. After a spell with Clacton he came to Halstead in 1954 with his family, Robert, junior, Patricia and Philip, as Player/Coach Manager and lived at the Nag's Head where he and his wife Dorothy ran the pub. He retired at the age of 42 and returned to his trade of a joiner. His son Robert was on the books of Southend and Colchester but left football to become a successful builder and owner of a golf club enabling his son Paul to become a professional golfer. Bob died in Halstead in 2001 in his 83rd year.

187. New Street in the early 1920s

No cardboard cartons from the supermarket in the days when this photo was taken. The milk was then delivered by pony and trap in churns from where it was ladled into the customer's own receptacle. Here we see the milkman in New Street c1920, outside the shop of Jonathan Taylor, at No. 40. He is listed in the town directories from the early 1890s as a shopkeeper and poultry dealer but later was classed as a druggist, selling a variety of "physic". This resulted in his schoolteacher daughter being nicknamed "Pills" Taylor.

I was told about one old time milkman, who went round with a horse and cart delivering milk from churns and who always wore a hat - a flat cap in the dry weather and a trilby when wet. It was realised after some time that rain collected in the brim of the latter and when he bent over to scoop the milk from the churn, the water ran off his hat straight into the milk. At the end of the day he managed to sell more milk than he started with.

FROM

ALFRED KEMP,

Painter, Plumber, Glazier, Sign Writer,
Paper Hanger & House Decorator.

New Street, HALSTEAD, Essex.

188. New Street pre 1905

A street scene you no longer see, a time when children could safely play in the road. The gas lamp was the centre of attraction here, an object that children ran round, climbed up and to where they tied their skipping ropes. The Gas Company was formed in 1835 but it was not until 1854 that the Rev. Charles Burney put forward a motion that the town be lighted with gas. To start with there were only 35 lamps dotted about which proved insufficient, and by 1900 the number had increased to 127. The next 50 years saw gas illumination disappearing in favour of electric, which took over completely in 1950. An anecdote related by Fred Simmons who left Halstead in 1874, recalled an incident that occurred when the gas supply was first installed into local houses. An old visitor to his home, unfamiliar with the service, blew out the gas and retired to bed. Smelling gas he tied his sock over the bracket to stop it escaping. Fortunately others arrived in time to avoid a tragedy. New Street was formerly called Berkley Terrace and before 1890 Brook Place was Johnson's Yard.

189. Community Centre, New Street, 1980

Early in 1943 the top half of the children's playing field beside the park and adjoining New Street was requisitioned by the Ministry of Works and Buildings, to erect a hostel. The Anglo-American Servicemen's Club was officially opened the following January, providing recreational facilities and refreshment for men in the forces and was run by the Y.M.C.A. with a full-time warden, assisted by local volunteers. In the early days of World War II a canteen had been run in the large schoolroom under the New Congregational Church in Parsonage Street (201). After the war the buildings stood empty for a while until being reused as Government offices - such as Ministry of Food, Labour Exchange, Customs & Excise, Pensions & National Insurance and the Forestry Commission. Halstead Urban District Council then purchased the property and transformed it into a Senior Citizens' Centre in 1972. Later it became a Community Centre and is now a meeting place for many local clubs and organisations.

190. New Street/Trinity Street, c1902

Before New Street existed, a large house stood on an expanse of land beside Chapel Street, now Trinity Street, near the present Police Station and was called Chapel House. During the first half of the 1800s it was the residence of doctors and surgeons, before they occupied Pitchards opposite. Dr C.G. Roberts, Medical Officer of Health, resided there before moving into Eastdene in 1905 which was built on the site of the large house and cottage in the photo. Local doctors had practises here until the mid 1900s.

The Methodist movement in Halstead was born in a house in Hedingham Lane (Road) in 1837, the home of Richard Taylor and seven years later the membership was 23. By 1846 the number had dropped to none and there was no mention of Methodists in the town until about 1861. That year services were revived and held in a hired room, until the members transferred to a rented barn in Trinity Road, registered as a place of worship and called the Preaching House. During the next ten years the members raised enough money to purchase part of a garden behind the house of Thomas Bell and abutted to New Street, on which to build their chapel. "The Primitive Methodist Church 1874" was inscribed on the foundation stone, but following Methodist Union an attempt was made to erase the word "Primitive" but it is still decipherable today. Music was provided by various harmoniums until 1960 when the pipe organ from the "Bung Chapel" (238) was acquired for £100, costing a further £350 to transfer and renovate. The Methodist Church can be seen in this view of New Street taken about 1902.

191. The fair in Raven's Meadow, 1965

Before the railway came to town in 1860 this field, now Raven's Meadow, at the junction of Parsonage Street and Balls Chase, was called Parson's Meadow. Where horses quietly graze today, it has been, for many years, a stop for travelling fairs and circuses, a football pitch and a venue where children were entertained with parties, sports and games, after parading through the town. It is a local joke that every time the fair arrives, the heavens will open for sure, making it very muddy under foot. Plans were passed in 1931 for a temporary shop to be erected in this corner of the field, selling confectionery and tobacco products, proving to be very popular. During World War II, a 24-hour guard was stationed here in case the enemy tried to infiltrate along the railway line, and in February 1944 the 1st Battn. Dorset Regiment gathered to be addressed by General Montgomery. Their headquarters was at Dynes Hall, where King George VI and "Monty" paid them a visit. The fire station was built in another corner of this field in 1968.

192. Halstead from Parsonage Street bridge

Pause at this spot today and you will see a completely different scene from this photo taken in the late 1800s. All that remains is Parsonage House by the river and St Andrew's Church. The spire that once graced the Congregational Church (201) was taken down after it became dangerous and all the little cottages in The Slate were demolished allowing the Secondary School, now Richard de Clare, to be extended. The large house, once called Clipt Hedges Villa, on the end of The Slate, unlike the other dwellings, faced the opposite way and had the postal address of Factory Terrace. Sometime in the past it was divided into two and the last occupants were Archie "Cuckoo" Gibbs, the local roadsweeper and his wife, with Ted and Beat Root in the other half. The little humpback bridge was replaced in 1909 then again in the 1960s when the road was widened. Parsonage House, reputed to be one of the oldest properties in the town, is believed to have been the original Parsonage house of the Rectory of Halstead, belonging to the Dean & Chapter of St Paul's Cathedral, London, who held the Rectory from 1274. A large tithe barn connected with it, stood on a piece of land nearby and for 600 years the Choral services at St Paul's were maintained by the tithes collected there. Centuries ago this area was called Barbicans End - a barbican was a tower or other fortification on an approach to a town, especially a gate or bridge - and was probably connected to Stanstead Hall estate which then reached down to the bridge. Shortly after World War II a crowd of excited children gathered in the narrow strip of meadowland between the river and the railway line, from where this photo was taken, to be entertained by a group of uniformed Cossacks, Russian cavalrymen, performing death defying tricks on horseback at breakneck speed.

193. Waterworks House and Pumping Station

As the demand for more pure water grew, a new well was sunk in 1890 and a pumping station built near the river in Parsonage Street. The well, 8½ feet in diameter and 69 ft deep, had a boring of 250 feet. The storage reservoir was enclosed in an ornamental brick tower, 60 ft high and holding 85,000 gallons in Colne Road (70), to where the water was pumped. The waterworks were officially handed over to the Local Board on March 2nd 1891, after which Mr George Courtauld turned on the steam to set the pumps in motion. Another tower was opened off Conies Road on December 16th 1967 to improve the water supply. The waterworks cottage (left), erected in 1892, was the first council built house and the first tenant was Arthur Symonds, the engine driver. He worked at Colne Road, taking over from his father, then moved to Parsonage Street, a position he held for 50 years.

In 1910, Councillor E.P. Morley moved a resolution that public baths were needed as several occupations were of a dirty nature and cleanliness was next to Godliness. Where there were 4,000 seats in places of worship, baths could be counted on one hand, forcing several locals to travel to Stisted on Sunday mornings to wash in public baths. Four months later a suggestion was put forward for baths to be erected near the water tower on Council's own land off Head Street, but a more central position was preferred. Mr George Courtauld gave £1,000 towards a swimming pool plus four slipper baths, opposite the waterworks, to commemorate the Coronation of King George V and Queen Mary. During the first four months a Swimming Club was formed and preparations were made for an Open Night. The dirty water was replaced by clean and seating was set up for spectators. Everything was practically ready when the swing doors flew open and in walked an uninvited guest, who promptly took a belly flop dive into the lovely clean water and swam a few lengths. There was no applause at the exhibition, just an urgent chase. The swimmer was forced to come out after being caught in a lifebelt - he was an escaped pig belonging to a local butcher.

194. Cottages in Parsonage Street in the mid 1900s

All this part of Parsonage Street has been demolished, along with nearly a hundred other cottages during the last century. The last to go were 98 & 100, which were left when the adjoining properties were removed. The end walls were made good with bricks salvaged from the clearance of Globe Yard, further up the road. These two were demolished many years later and replaced by two new houses facing Gardener's Road. The photo was taken before 1966 when the road was widened.

Just round the corner on the left of these houses was The Slate (192) where in 1897 a rent free cottage, one room up and down, was given for a Mission by Mr Dunt. He repaired and painted it at his own expense and at the grand opening 25 people sat down to tea. Two meetings a week were held there and a Bible Class on Thursdays.

195. Parsonage Street in the mid 1900s

The Griffin, right, is one of the few pubs to have survived many years in Halstead. During the 1860s, one licensee, T. King, a brewer and maltster, brewed his own beer to sell at the lowest possible prices - "from 6d (2½p) to 1/2d (6p) per gallon or 3½d (1½p) per pot if the customer brought his own jug". The next building up the hill was another pub called "The Gardener's Arms", which lost its licence in 1923. When the Town bridge (15) was being widened in 1912, workmen unearthed an old spoon dated 1757 and marked "M.G.". It was thought to have been the property of Mark Gardener, who once held the licence of the pub - was it named after him? On the bowl of the spoon was the sign of the Gardener's Arms - a five-bar gate crossed with a range of gardening tools. The property was sold to Charlie Coe in 1924 plus a market garden and orchard at the rear, the produce from which he sold in the shop and hawked around the neighbourhood. The ex pub and cottages were demolished to make way for the Gardener's Road development in the early 1960s.

196. The Globe in the early 1930s

This photo of the Globe was taken after 1930 when this building replaced an earlier pub of the same name. The old cottages, on the left side, were demolished at a later date. A pathway from Parsonage Street, down the right side of the pub led to Globe Yard where an old cotton winding mill stood. At one time the manufacture of silk ribbons was carried on here too, by a Mr Foster, followed by the making of blankets and shawls for a short time. The factory closed and was partitioned off to make five or six dwelling houses. A report dated 1893 states that Dr Roberts complained that he had to wade through water in the back kitchens of these cottages. Maybe the water came from a spring or well that Parsonage Street or Lane, as it was known, was noted for. In fact I was told of one well in that vicinity that was not discovered when new houses were built on the site.

197. The remains of Victoria Hall in 1906

On Christmas Eve 1893 a Bible Class met for the first time in an old cottage in Parsonage Street, when 33 people were present. Numbers increased so much that George Tyler, founder of the club, purchased the block of cottages. Four years later membership had risen to 350, far too many for the space available, so Victoria Hall was erected at the rear and opened in December 1897 when 700 people attended. A disastrous fire broke out on November 23rd 1906, completely destroying the club and hall, leaving a mangled mess seen in the photo. At the time the club premises were used for teas and storage of furniture ready for a sale in the hall. The Volunteer Fire Brigade was summonsed but neither the hall or club could be saved as all the available water had to be used to stop the fire spreading to surrounding cottages. All this occurred on the site of 42/44 Parsonage Street, the homes of Joyce and Mary to whom this book is dedicated, where twelve weavers' cottages originally stood. There were more of these homes situated between Parsonage Street and Colchester Road now Mallows Field, on an area called Knaves Acre Row.

198. The Salvation Army Citadel, Parsonage Street

Today's headquarters of the Joshua Nunn Lodge of the Freemasons has had various uses during its history, starting life in 1893 as the Salvation Army Citadel, with seating for 300 people. Unfortunately lack of finances forced the Army to vacate the building in 1910, when it was acquired by Mr S.G. Tyler for his Bible Class. An extension was added at the rear and after a complete overhaul it was reopened on June 5th 1910 as St Andrew's Hall by F.A.Vaizey. His father, J.A. Vaizey had performed the same ceremony in respect of Victoria Hall (197) eighteen years previous. The Electric Kinema was accommodated here from 1913 and run by Tom Keneally, who went about his business in a donkey cart. He closed his cinema in 1916 to become manager of the Empire (28). The Salvation Army re-established its headquarters in May 1929. Nine years later the Junior Imperial League took over the hall whereupon the name changed to the Imperial Hall. Troops were billeted here during World War II and later the property was bought by Courtaulds. Another change occurred in 1953 when it became the Central Accounts Office for Thomas Moy Ltd, coal and builders merchants. They ceased using this building circa 1970, after which it became the Masonic Hall.

199. The White Horse, Parsonage Street

Now a private residence this public house, The White Horse, had its own brewery in 1780 with equipment valued at £700 - a considerable amount in those days. It was here that George Cook was taught to brew by a relative in 1870, before spending a short time at Goslings Brewery in Bocking, to where he walked every day. He then acquired another job in Halstead brewing for George Burford at 41 Chapel Hill, a former Inland Revenue Officer. In 1885 George took up the challenge to brew his own beer so he rented 105 Parsonage Street, next door to the Griffin, and converted the adjoining maltings. His output was about ten barrels weekly, sold mainly to farmers to quench the thirst of their farm labourers. The seed was sown that gradually grew into a family run business that was established on Tidings Hill by his son George E. Cook (227). The maltings were bought by the Council in 1949 and demolished to make way for the Courtauld Close development. In 1863 there were at least 31 inns and beerhouses in the town but although the population has doubled since those days, the number of pubs has dropped to twelve, due to so many other outlets for alcoholic drinks.

200. White Horse Yard in the 1930s

Evelyn Bearman and little Margaret Waring are seen here standing outside a cottage in White Horse Yard. In the early 1800s there were at least four cottages at right-angles to the rear of the pub, with access on the right. Demolition took place when the pub was enlarged in 1937/8 when only two of them were left. On June 21st 1897 land was set apart as a playground for youngsters to commemorate Queen Victoria's long reign and called "Children's Piece". It was a gift of the Rev T.G. Gibbons that "children might enjoy the fresh air and have a place to play in where they would be in safety". It was for under 13 year olds living in the vicinity, but adults and young people could use it as long as they did not disturb the "happiness of the little ones". Access was through White Horse Yard and "not over the fence from Globe Yard". Unfortunately there was a disagreement between the reverend gentleman and the ratepayers over the upkeep of the fencing and a few months later he closed the playground, selling part of the land to an adjoining property owner. There was a dispute over the land in 1939, whether it had been legally dedicated to the public. The answer came from Stanley Moger who stated "it was to have been made public if Halstead children behaved themselves but they never did so they didn't get it". For a time in the early 1900s S.G. Pudney, a polisher and upholsterer, had a workshop in the yard where he remade and cleaned mattresses.

201. New Congregational Church with Old Independent Meeting Burial Ground

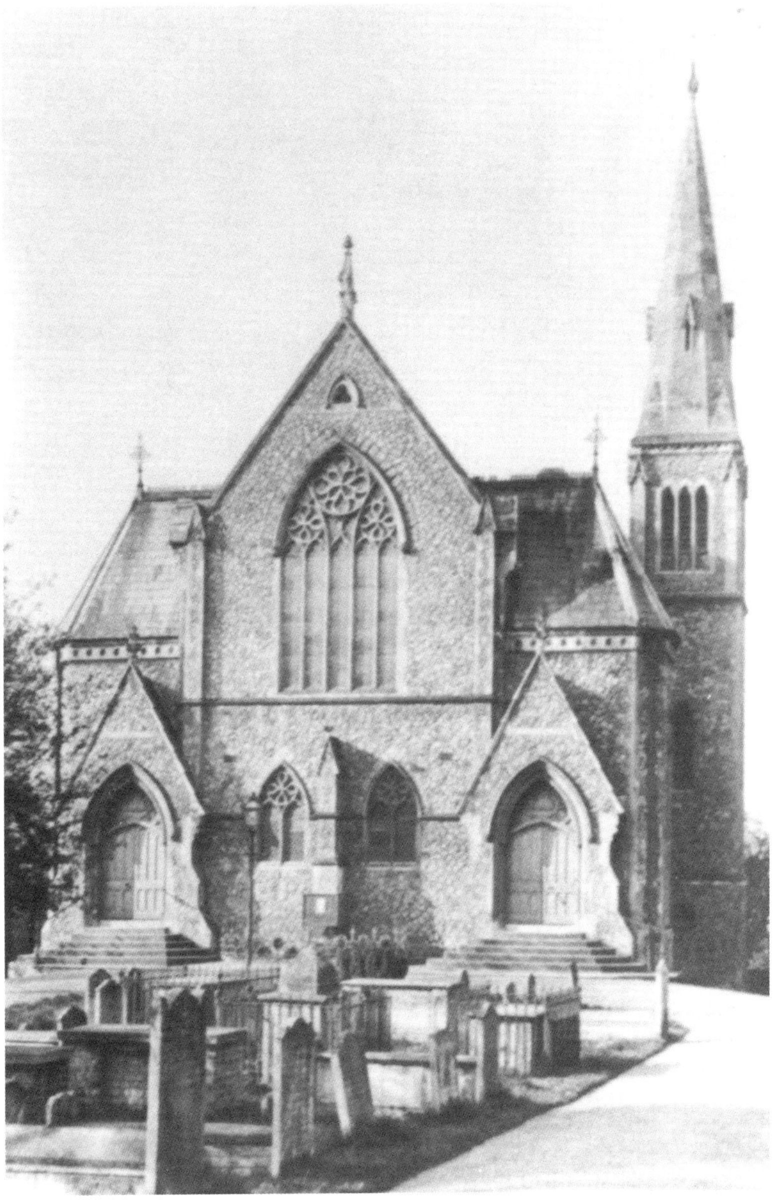

After the ejection of Rev Wm. Sparrow from St Andrew's Church on the passing of the Act of Uniformity, lectures were held in a barn behind the White Hart (136). These proved very popular and the congregations increased. Consequently in 1679 the first Independent Meeting House was erected on this spot in Parsonage Street. A second building took its place in 1718 when the congregation numbered 500 people. The new church was erected some distance from the road, behind a row of cottages, as the law forbade Dissenter's properties to front a roadway. The seating was supervised, only subscribers to the minister were allowed pews in the body of the church and the building subscribers had the privilege of seats in the front gallery for their maidservants. Between 1748 and 1756 pew rents ranged from 1/- (5p) to 4/- (20p) and those paying the least had to move if a higher price was offered. In March 1865 the last service took place and the foundation stone of the New Congregational Church was laid on August 29th 1865. The tombstones on the Old Independent burial ground at the front of the church were removed and placed along the boundary of the land and a Garden of Remembrance laid out with lawns and roses. Sadly problems arose with the building and its spire but repairs were too costly, resulting in a losing battle. On Easter Sunday, March 30th 1997 the last service was held, ending worship on this site after 335 years. It is recorded that near the Old Independent Chapel was a well called Holy Well or Hollow Well and that a lane called Holy Lane ran from Parsonage Street down the back of the High Street.

202. Parsonage Street cottages in the mid 1900s

Behind these cottages and to the right, on land between Parsonage Street, Mallows Field and Colchester Road stood many dwellings connected to the home weaving industry. Most were demolished when Stanley Moger started his market (59) and an article written in 1890 states that "a place, which now bears the dignified title of Garden Court was in former times familiarly known as Kicking Dickey Square, from the possible fact that a beerhouse sign of the Kicking Dickey existed". Is this referring to these dwellings as there was a large garden in that area where a row of houses were erected called Garden Terrace? The two cottages on the extreme right which still remain, once stood at the entrance to Moon, originally Moonshiney Yard. A very old house called Moonshiney Hall was situated in Colchester Road behind the cottages in the photo.

On the left, a double-fronted house was the home and business of the Frye family. Mr & Mrs Frye ran a drapery and the daughter gave piano lessons.

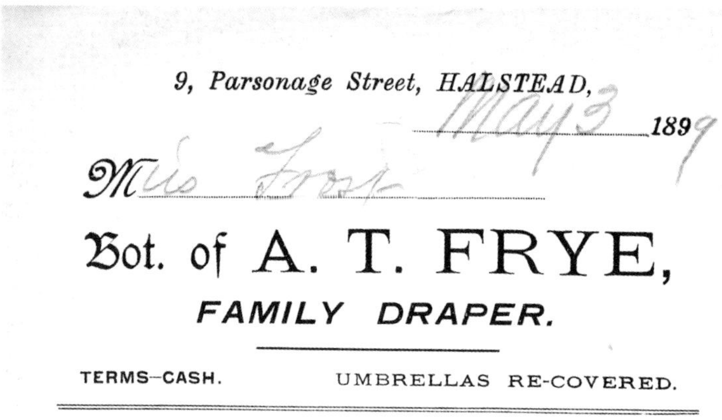

9, Parsonage Street, HALSTEAD,

May 3 1899

M

Bot. of A. T. FRYE,

FAMILY DRAPER.

TERMS—CASH. UMBRELLAS RE-COVERED.

203. St Andrew's Vicarage pre 1915

Erected in 1875 on the site of an earlier vicarage, this large 22 roomed house was demolished 99 years later, when it became too large for today's requirements. Much of the material was salvaged and used in the present vicarage, the third to be built on the site. Fanny Burney, authoress and daughter of Dr Charles Burney, an English composer, used to stay at the old vicarage with her relation the Rev John Hawkins, vicar from 1792-1804. She died in 1840 three years before another relative, the Rev Charles Burney became the first vicar of Holy Trinity. A year later he was installed as vicar at the newly built St James church at Greenstead Green, before moving to St Andrew's, where he remained for fourteen years. He was responsible for building the Vicarage School for his wife in 1861/2. This was demolished in 1923 and St Andrew's Hall, designed by Duncan Clark, a local man, erected on the site. At the rear of the hall, a retiring room and kitchen above extensive stores were known as the old Vicarage School and on the outside of the south wall is a brick, partially hidden behind a drainpipe, inscribed "Mrs B. 1861", referring to Mrs Burney and her school. Fanny Burney and her book 'Evelina' are commemorated on Courtauld houses in the town (115).

204. Outside the Manse, Parsonage Street, c1900

I have no idea what the occasion was but this small crowd are all waiting for something to happen outside The Manse, with every one of them wearing a hat. In 1873, the Rev. Samuel Parkinson became the minister of the New Congregational Church but the old Parsonage had fallen into disrepair, making it unsuitable for his large family. It was demolished and this Manse built for him at a cost of £800 in 1875. In those days the stipend was sufficient for him to support a large family and servants. Records refer to congregations of 1,000 people, with a Sunday School of 400 children taught by 28 teachers. The Rev. Parkinson resided at the Manse for over 30 years retiring in 1907. The house was sold in 1956 as it was too large for the smaller families and Waverley House in Colchester Road was purchased for the Manse. To the right of the Manse is No. 12 where John Harvey started his saddlery business.

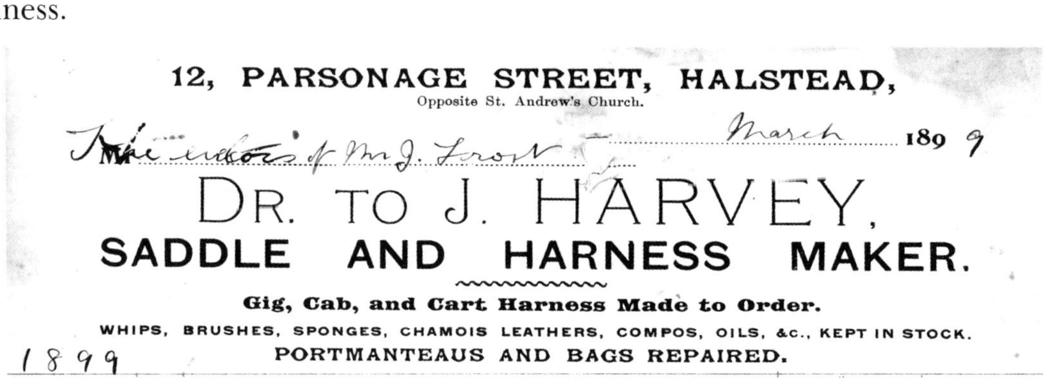

12, PARSONAGE STREET, HALSTEAD,

Opposite St. Andrew's Church.

The creditors of Mr J. Frost March 1899

DR. TO J. HARVEY,

SADDLE AND HARNESS MAKER.

Gig, Cab, and Cart Harness Made to Order.

WHIPS, BRUSHES, SPONGES, CHAMOIS LEATHERS, COMPOS, OILS, &c., KEPT IN STOCK.

1899 PORTMANTEAUS AND BAGS REPAIRED.

205. Parson's Yard, Parsonage Street, early 1900s

Another of Halstead's numerous yards, lined with little cottages was Parson's Yard, situated between 10 and 12 Parsonage Street. Here we are standing in the yard looking out towards the church. The bike is leaning against a wall where there was a shop. It was here that my grandfather, John Harvey, started his saddlery business at No. 12 in 1899, eventually moving to 11 Hedingham Road in 1916. Before the days of MFI, etc, all furniture was hand made to order and one cabinet maker, employing a few men, was Caleb Beckwith, whose workshop was at the bottom of this yard. Besides being a furniture maker and upholsterer, he was also an undertaker.

MEMORANDUM.

FROM **CALEB ∻ BECKWITH,**
CABINET ✣ MAKER,
Upholsterer, French Polisher and Undertaker,
PARSONAGE STREET & HIGHFIELD PLACE,
COLCHESTER ROAD, HALSTEAD, ESSEX.

July 24 1900
To Mr Edmd Frost
Halstead

MANUFACTURER OF CHURCH AND SCHOOL FURNITURE.

~~~~~~~~~~~~~~~~~~~~~~~

206. Parsonage Street in 1965

Hardly any changes have occurred in this part of old Halstead since this photo was taken. How many remember "Grandma's", the business that opened at No. 4 about 1970, when Anne Hugessen Ltd started a venture manufacturing a wide range of leather goods. The firm hit the headlines when they mass produced chastity belts, selling them worldwide - some even found their way to the Virgin Isles! Shortly after transferring to the Bluebridge Industrial Estate in 1974 the firm collapsed. One popular little shop was the Chocolate Box at No. 10, a bread and cake shop where customers could go through to a back room to sit and chat with a snack and a 'cuppa'. The entrance to Parsonage Street was at one time extremely narrow and a cottage is said to have been demolished enabling the road to be widened - was this part of the old Dolphin (129)?
~~~~~~~~~~~~~~~~~~~~~~~

PRETORIA ROAD

207. Pretoria Road, in 1977

The present day Jehovah's Witness, Kingdom Hall, at the lower end of Pretoria Road, was originally the Drill Hall built for the Territorial Army and opened in 1925. The hall was wired ready for electric power, unavailable at the time, so a temporary supply of gas was installed for the lighting and heat was obtained from a large Tortoise Stove (216).

Further up Pretoria Road at its junction with Morley Road stands a detached house that Mrs W.J. Courtauld, of Penny Pot, had built and furnished. It was opened by her on April 2nd 1924 as a home for the District Nurse who held a surgery there every Tuesday from 7-9pm. Two nurses were employed by the Nursing Association, one attended to maternity cases and the other to general cases.

When this road was under construction Pretoria was taken from the Dutch during the Boer War so the name was given to commemorate the occasion. After a while the Council changed their minds and thought it would be nicer to name it after the gentleman who had owned the property - Vaizey or even Attwoods that had Vaizey connections. It was finally decided that the Council had no right to alter the name so Pretoria Road was taken over by the Council on April 1st 1901.

208. The Arms of the Railway

Several influential local gentlemen met at The Howe (118), then the home of Edward Hornor, in the mid 1850s. It was at this meeting that they agreed to start a Railway Company, resulting in the birth of the Colne Valley & Halstead Railway Company. The 'first sod' was cut in February 1858 by James Brewster, near Elms Hall, resulting in the Chappel to Halstead 'iron road' opening in 1860. The following year it had extended to Hedingham and ten months later reached as far as Great Yeldham, opening on May 26th 1862. The final section to Haverhill was completed with the first train using the line on May 10th 1863. The Company lost its separate identity when merging with the London & North Eastern Railway Company in 1923. It was then that a shield bearing the Arms (above) was presented to the Halstead Urban District Council. It depicts the Essex Arms at the top, the old Halstead Arms (125) on the left and the Colne Valley to the right. This Coat of Arms was for many years depicted on the sign of the Colne Valley Arms public house at Birdbrook.

209. An early view of the Railway Station

With no signal box or goods yard this photograph is a very early look at the Railway Station, probably 1877. Behind the engine are three goods trucks, two carriages and the guard's van. The carriages were some of the original Colne Valley stock, with straight sides and very low roofs, where passengers sat on seats round the walls, not across the carriage. The wooden fences in the foreground bordered a rough lane, then known as Railway Road, previously called New Road. It was officially named Kings Road in 1890. This area is now Trinity Court looking from the park.

THE

COLNE VALLEY

and

HALSTEAD

RAILWAY

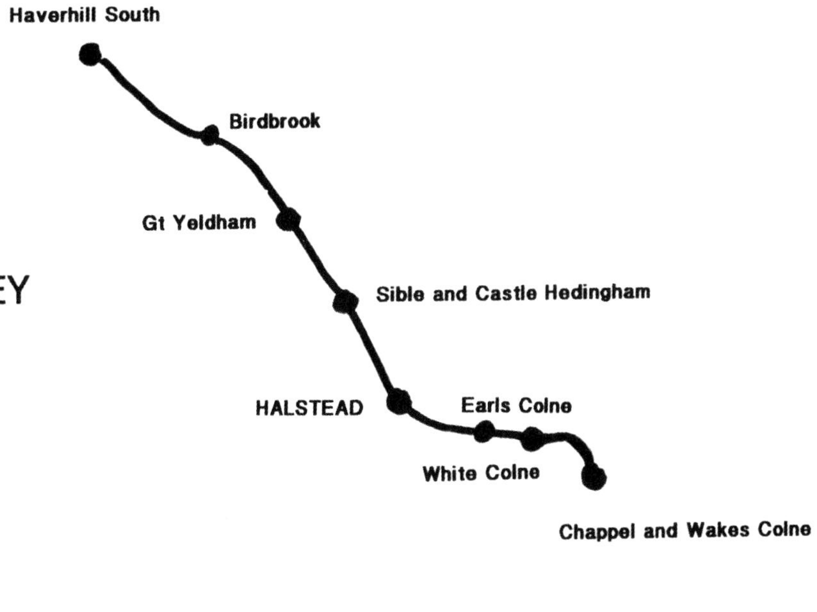

210. Halstead Station in the late 1800s

Halstead Station was erected in 1862 by Rayner & Runnacles, in readiness for the Agricultural Society's Show held at Sloe House (220). The same firm was responsible for the long wooden footbridge spanning the railway, which was erected in five weeks at a cost of £160 and can be seen in the background. The station looks deserted here but it was a very different story one Saturday in June 1899. On that day several hundred Courtauld factory employees paid a visit to Yarmouth, along with 120 from the Tortoise Works. On the same excursion there were 45 from Rippers joinery works and all Walter Clark's workmen. The train of twenty coaches was pulled by two engines, the journey taking three hours. On the same day 120 New Congregational Sunday School scholars with teachers, parents and friends visited Clacton by road. This trip to the sea took 3½ hours, longer than the train time. The mass exodus must have left the town very quiet and empty. Trinity Court now occupies this site.

211. Halstead Railway Station, c1920

Standing on this spot today you are looking at Trinity Court but if you had been here in the 1850s the scene would then have been many cottages. As the Colne Valley & Halstead Railway was being constructed at that time, a compulsory purchase order was made to acquire land for the building of the railway, station and goods yard. With the granting of this order 152 cottages were demolished, resulting "in 608 labouring classes being thrown on the street overnight". A note added to the order remarks, "No inconvenience anticipated". Where on earth did all those poor people go? A beerhouse keeper, William Cook (103) was the owner of the land and property, including his own large house that once belonged to Wm. Martin, a charitable man. All this was purchased for £1,000, for the building of the station platform, buildings and forecourt. William bought and built many cottages in the town - was this to re-house all those made homeless? The engine standing in the station was built in 1887 and was named "Halstead", later known as No. 2.

212. The last days of the Colne Valley Railway

From the Iron Footbridge (213), looking towards Trinity Street, we see a deserted railway station and goods yard at the end of its life. The last passenger train left on December 31st 1961, but a restricted goods service continued until the end of 1964, finally closing in April 1965. When the line opened to Hedingham in July 1861 cheap fares were offered - 4d (1½p) return. As a result 1,700 people took advantage of this, so many that cattle trucks had to be used to carry them all. The following stories with railway connections were told by Stan Randall, a well-loved reporter of the Halstead Gazette for 50 years. Pranks were carried out by Earls Colne Grammar school boys who travelled on the train to school each day in the early 1900s. One day they drilled a small hole through the partition into the next compartment and after waiting several days at last spied a passenger seated in front of the hole, just waiting to be sprayed with ink from a fountain pen. The dastardly deed was carried out just as the train pulled to a halt at Halstead station, enabling the boys to get out of the train on the wrong side and beat a hasty retreat across the goods yard.

It was a long trek from the school to Earls Colne station and the boys were allowed just enough time to walk back for the return journey. On games afternoons they had to walk an extra ½ mile. Time after time the train would be moving off as they belted down to the station, where fellow students would be waiting with doors thrown open for the boys to literally fall into the carriages. This was a dangerous practice and one day as they came charging down the hill a burly porter blocked their way and would not allow them onto the platform. While they were contemplating whether to wait three hours for the next train or walk home, a couple of railwaymen arrived at the crossing gates on the Halstead side on a manually propelled platelayer's trolley. The men dismounted and proceeded to open the gates and as they did so several of the boys made a dash for the trolley and with two boys pumping the propelling handles and others pushing, they were away down the line to Halstead. Never before had one of those sedate vehicles been pushed along so fast as that one, but with the journey half completed came an unforeseen problem - the gates at Langley Mill were closed against them. It was realised that the gatekeeper would be in his little hut beside the line so they had to abandon the trolley and walk the rest of the way home by the riverbank. The next morning the headmaster was waiting for the "train boys" together with Mr Hawkins, manager of the Colne Valley Railway from 1903-1923, who duly stayed to see the ringleaders well and truly walloped. No doubt they decided to walk the next time.

In 1972, local railway enthusiasts formed the Preservation Society at Castle Hedingham where much of the railway lives on.

212a These men are the station staff of Halstead posing in the early years of the 20th century.

Front Row left to right: C. Pavely, F. Cook, H. Wiffen, F. Coppin (Stationmaster), J. Miller, A. Harrington and S. Norfolk.

Back row: T. Benham, J. Pafflin, E. Dixey, A. Eves, D. Amos, A. Cansell and F. Hart

213. The end of the Colne Valley Railway, 1965

Another view taken in 1965 looking in the opposite direction, from a spot now the electric motor factory, quite different from what we see today. The iron footbridge over the railway was erected about 1904 and demolished in 1965, being replaced by Factory Lane West. The tall chimney attached to Courtauld's powerhouse built in 1922 can be seen on the left, before being removed 48 years later. Plans were passed in 1949 for the silo erected the following year in a siding for Newman & Clark. It was 90 ft high and graced the skyline for 50 years. It was knocked down, with great difficulty, to make way for the Dr Elizabeth Courtauld Surgery, opened in August 2000. Dr Elizabeth was one of the first lady doctors in the country and was born in 1867 at Cut Hedge, now Gosfield School. Also she funded the building of an outpatients block at Halstead Hospital, founded by her father in 1884. The houses on the right are in Kings Road.

Remainders of the railway are Parsonage Street gate-house, the Tarpaulin shop, now Andrew's pharmacy, the station master's office and the base of the water tank near the United Reformed Church and an old carriage at North Mills (175) purchased by Edmund Frost in 1910/11 and pulled up the hill by eight horses to serve as a playroom for his children.

214. The Co-op Yard, 1967

Riverside Court is certainly more pleasing to the eye than this area used to be. The site, on which the flats stand, was latterly referred to as the Co-op yard and over the years has had many changes. During the late 1800s there was a large garden complete with greenhouse, that belonged to a florist and a variety of other trades have been run in sheds of all sizes. One of the early trades was rope-making, carried out in the large boarded building, then lying parallel with Rosemary Lane. It began life as a ropewalk and at one time belonged to William Spurgeon, who rented it out for many years. I am sure this has seen more changes of use than any other premises in the town - here are just a few. The Salvation Army established itself there, in spite of opposition, in the mid 1880s, after first holding a meeting in the Railway Station yard opposite, eventually transferring to Parsonage Street (198) in 1893. The Halstead Gazette then moved in for a short time, followed by the Colne Valley Printing Co. On March 27th 1898 the local members of the Roman Catholic Church went from worshipping in a private house to the old ropewalk, but this venture was short-lived, leaving it vacant for the Conservative Club to move in from the High Street, eventually going to its present day location. Again in 1910, the Salvation Army acquired the premises after being "turned out on the street" from the Imperial Hall (198) and from here supplied foundry workers and other "early birds" with early morning refreshments. Ned Cant also rented the building for a while, where furniture was sold on the ground floor and soft furnishings made upstairs. In a separate workshop nearby he made furniture. The Co-op purchased the whole area, then called Goodey's Yard in 1937, at the same time that the Eastern National bus company, who garaged their buses in the yard, moved to the High Street (154). Lock-up garages were erected by the Co-op in 1955 as there was great demand, due to the lack of garage facilities at most houses. The photo shows the area in 1967, with the old ropewalk on the right and Clover's Mill (20) in the background.

215. Charles Portway (1828-1909)

Charles Portway was born in Bury St Edmunds in 1828 and when he was 23, purchased an ironmongers business in the High Street (147), and soon became very successful. Charles wanted to heat his bitterly cold warehouse, so he designed and made his first Tortoise Stove. In 1878 he was joined by Harry, his son, and about the same time brought out and patented his stove. The demand was so great from his friends and neighbouring shopkeepers that they found it necessary to purchase the old Colne Valley Ironworks in Rosemary Lane, that had been lying idle for some time. This was opened as a foundry and manufacturing works called the Tortoise Works. Charles took a very active part in the Town's affairs. He was President of the Liberal Association and entertained Herbert Asquith, the Prime Minister, at his residence, The Croft (147). He was a staunch churchman and took great interest in all public works, education and sport, holding numerous offices. He was largely instrumental in obtaining the Recreational Ground for the town and donated the bandstand. A man who lived his life in the fast lane - unlike the tortoise! He died in 1909 aged 80 years.

216. Inside the Tortoise Works

The photo shows the inside of the Tortoise Works with stoves in various stages. From 1877-1890 more than 100,000 were manufactured, demonstrating how popular they were. "Slow but sure", was the motto of the stove that was invented to give out the maximum heat from the least fuel, into the room and not up the chimney. They were constructed in various forms to heat anything from halls, greenhouses, bedrooms, barracks to churches "perfect in action, clean, safe and economical". In 1882 the firm moved into a former foundry premises in Rosemary Lane. As well as stoves they cast supports for school desks, barley twist edgings for gardens, fences, gates, mantelpieces, carriage jacks, coke-breakers, etc. In 1889 2,000 iron chairs for the French Exhibition were completed in 14 days. Taylor and Portway's are still involved in the heating industry on the Broton Estate, not far from the original works, with the Portway family still playing an active part. The Tortoise Stove ceased production completely in 1999 and in all its history had not changed in any way.

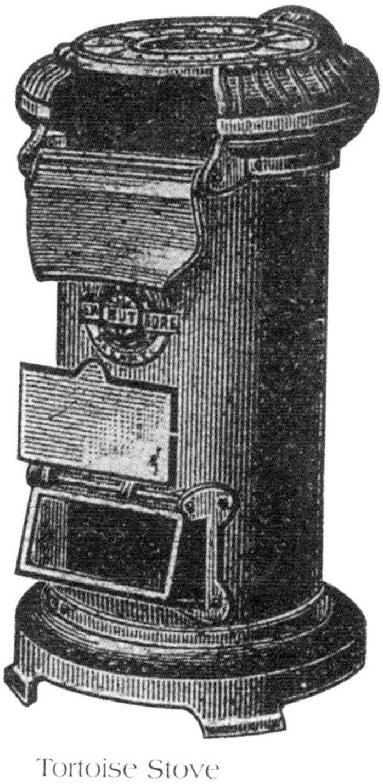

Tortoise Stove

217. Halstead Town Football team, 1948

Halstead Town Football Club was officially opened on August 21st 1948, after months of mostly voluntary work to produce a fine football pitch at Rosemary Lane. The club was founded in 1879, but never had a permanent ground, using fields in various parts of the town, and at one time used the land that became Kings Road playing field. In 1947, when Halstead won the Essex Junior Cup, it was decided that they should have a ground of their own and the meadow next to the Tortoise Bowling Green gave the best prospects and was offered by S.A. Courtauld on suitable terms, enabling a three year plan to be set in motion. The first year the meadow was developed as there was a pit that had to be filled in and a large ditch piped. The second year saw the provision of dressing-rooms, with baths for the players and thirdly the erection of the stand, opened in 1950. The team in the photo played at the opening match on the new pitch, against Eton Manor, the team they had beaten in the Cup match, but this time the tables were turned. The oldest surviving former player, Harry Rayner, aged 78, kicked off, having joined the team in 1888, when they played at Coggeshall Pieces. The line-up:

Back Row l-r : Bert Everitt (referee), Ken Dollin, Jock Spiers, Roy Charlton, Bill Cornell, Mick Osborne, Vic Arnold and Bert Johnson (linesman).

Front Row : Johnnie Webber, John Dakin, Jimmy Wilson, Innes Murray and Bob Barker with Ray Osborne (Mascot) with the ball.

218. Highwoods farmyard in 1921

Here we see Mr & Mrs Baker in the yard at Highwoods Farm off Russells Road, fattening up the turkeys for Christmas. Lewis Baker, a Welsh sheep farmer came to Halstead in 1916 to try his hand at arable farming and stock breeding, succeeded and stayed there with his wife Cecelia and family.

In a survey of the manor of Blampsters (sic) taken in 1565, there is mention of a lane called Russels Lane running from above Blampster's Oak leaving the Braintree road on the town side of what is now Attwoods, then on to White Horse Green now White Ash Green via Russells Farm. Blampster's Oak was a large tree that stood on wasteland near the entrance to Oak Road and near the Blamster's Farm gate, an area then referred to as Three Lane's End. In the early 1800s, when the Lord of the Manor, the Earl of Mornington, wanted to cut down this magnificent tree with a trunk measuring 18ft in circumference, there was a public outcry. A lawyer was instructed to obtain an injunction to protect the "Monarch of the Woods" but unfortunately there were no quick means of communication in those days so by the time the triumphant opponents returned with the necessary papers the tree had already been felled.

Nearby, Attwoods was built in 1814 by the grandfather of R.E. Vaizey, on a site originally occupied by an old farmhouse, when all the surrounding land was covered in woods - from where the residence took its name.

219. Sloe Hill, c1910

Sloe Hill has had a variety of names - Gosfield Road, Greenwood Hill, Deacon's Hill and now Sloe Hill. The photo shows a very narrow lane, once described as "a strip of road that presented a surface like a ploughed field", without footpaths. Nearly 20 years later Mrs C.C. Courtauld of Penny Pot was concerned about all the unemployment in the town and offered to help ease the situation with a gift of £2,500 to meet the cost of road improvements. It was given on condition that the workforce was changed every fortnight to give as many unemployed as possible a little pocket money for Christmas. The widening of the road took place from the Bird in Hand to a point just below Sloe House. Parts of the highway near the Plantation, on the left, were only 17ft wide before being increased to 30ft plus footpaths. The improvements gave work to 27 men weekly. Before the houses were built on the right-hand side in the 1930s the area at the top of the bank was allotments. The Plantation (left) was occupied by the army during World War II but unfortunately a few years later many beech trees died, probably due to the petrol and oil from army lorries soaking through the soil.

Over a century ago, at the bottom of Sloe Hill, beside the path leading through the Plantation to Russells Road, stood a poplar tree with a circumference of 12 feet and extremely tall - said to have attracted the attention of many passers-by and was easily the tallest of its kind in the district. Another proof of the fertility of the soil in the Crowbridge area.

220. Sloe House in the 1980s

The site on which this handsome country mansion stands at the top of Sloe Hill, was held in Saxon times by Wulfwine, from whom it was taken and given to Aubrey de Vere by William the Conqueror. Aubrey was married to Beatrix, half-sister of William and was an ancestor of the Earls of Oxford - the De Veres, a family reputed to be one of the most ancient and famous families in the world, producing a succession of twenty Earls during 1137-1703. The estate had several owners including John de Bousser (Bourchier), whose descendant Bartholomew made it part of the endowment of the Chantry in the High Street. James Sparrow became the owner in 1698, before Charles Hanbury pulled down the old manor and replaced it with the present day house. The first Essex Show was held in the grounds by kind permission of Robert E. Greenwood in 1862, and during World War II Sloe House was commandeered by the War Office to serve as Headquarters of the Special Air Service and the Royal Signals where there was a section of homing pigeons used for communications.

Summer Garden Parties were started in 1890 to entertain workers and their families on Wednesdays - early closing day. The parties commenced at 5.30pm until 9.00pm, when there was music by the Town Band and dancing on the lawns of many local large houses. Sloe House was one of these venues along with The Howe, The Croft, Ashford Lodge, Star Stile, Gosfield Place, Attwoods, Cut Hedge, Dynes Hall, Greenstead Hall, Nether Priors, The Cedars, Firwoods and St Andrew's Vicarage. There was an admission fee of 2d (1p) and hundreds attended. After ten years these events came to an end and it was then that Mr W.C. Sheen started annual tradesmen's excursions to Clacton on the train to take their place. In August 1901 one trip carried 870 passengers taking advantage of the offer.

221. A sketch of part of Golden Meadow Camp by a German prisoner

As you walk or drive out of the town on the Sudbury Road, you pass a large field on the right, between the cricket ground and Ashford Lodge - a quiet location, but not always so. One afternoon in 1891 nearly a thousand excited people made their way on foot and in traps to witness a horse race that had been the talk of the town. Charles Hearn and George Smith had challenged each other to a race. At the appointed hour neither had arrived, but 20 minutes later Charles' horse appeared, so it was decided to send it over the course - four times round the field. The jockey donned his colours and with the aid of six men mounted the horse. The official starter also failed to turn up so Mr Plummer, from Bentall's opposite, took on the duty. The first time round, when he arrived at "Tattenham Corner", the horse stopped to look down the road to see if Mr Smith was coming. On coming round to the starting point for the first time it ran into the crowd and then the real fun started. The way in which some of the spectators jumped over the hedges was unforgettable. The horse repeated this each time it came round, obviously enjoying itself before finishing. There were people from all the surrounding villages and one man travelled all the way from London to witness the spectacle - Halstead's One Horse Race.

More excitement prevailed when Charles W. Bragg descended in an aeroplane on the meadow in 1918 to visit his home. The descent was easy but when he tried to take off trouble arose. A strong gust of wind blew just as he took off, causing the plane to hit some high trees and crash to the ground. The woodwork of the craft was severely damaged but the rest suffered very little. Needless to say a large crowd soon collected and a guard of Special Constables was put on watch until a party arrived to dismantle the machine to take it away. What happened to the pilot? Was he confined to barracks or court-martialled? No, he was promoted and put on a "bombing machine". He went on to receive a commission in the R.A.F., survived a serious motor-cycle accident, then sadly was killed at the age of 26 years when ironically the wind caught his aircraft, causing it to nosedive and burst into flames on impact.

In 1921 the meadow was used as the starting place for pleasure flights of five minutes duration and cost 10/6d (52½p). Men, women and children made the trip - anyone over the age of 85 went free. Two decades later this field was covered by nissen huts - Golden Meadow Camp for Prisoners of War. Originally built during World War II by the Americans and occupied by them until 1944, when about 500 Italians were held there, followed by the Germans. Many of the prisoners helped out on local farms and after the War stayed in the area, marrying local girls. After all the prisoners had left in 1948, many local families squatted in the huts due to a housing shortage. As each family was rehoused the hut in which they had lived was demolished and gradually the whole area returned to the peaceful field we see today, with just one reminder - remnants of the concrete entrance can still be seen on the roadside.

Further up the Sudbury road, on the right, stands Ashford Lodge. William J. Evans states in "Old and New Halstead" published in 1886 that the large house was built by Firmin de Tastet, "who went to great expense in improving the roadway in front of the house". One recorded memory of an old Halsteadian states that the road passed so near that those riding in coaches could almost touch the windows. The gentleman must have paid to have a new road constructed further away, accounting for the straight stretch in that area today. In November 1922 Charles Rayner arrived with Claude Reeve to sweep the chimneys and clean the boilers. On entering the roof he was aware that something was smouldering which was ignited by the draught and soon the whole roof was alight. Staff tried to put the fire out but no amount of buckets of water would quell it. The Halstead Volunteer Fire Brigade eventually arrived after having to physically pull the engine to the location as the contract lorry was unavailable. Unfortunately an adequate water supply could not be set up, resulting in the whole interior being destroyed, leaving only the walls. It was rebuilt as we see it today.

222. Ready, Steady, Go!

Taken at the junction of Sudbury Road and Star Stile, on July 31st 1890, this photo records the start of a paperchase on cycles, by suitably attired young men - no anti-litter laws in those days. The 'hares', with their bags of paper pieces, T. Bate and F. Fitch, were despatched by the timekeeper and fifteen 'hounds' followed five minutes later. The course taken was up Sudbury Road, through Wickham St Pauls and back to Halstead, covering a distance of 16 miles. The 'hares' finished in 1 hour 23 mins., closely followed by the 'hounds' who arrived one minute later. The next year a meeting was held at the George Hotel (127) to consider forming a cycling club. It was decided to form one at once, to be called Halstead Cycling Club. Note there are no lady riders in the photo. I read of one well-known Gosfield lady who, on the introduction of the bicycle, learnt to ride secretly at Attwoods, as her father did not think it right or proper for young ladies to ride on the machine. By 1894 the club had 42 members, with lady cyclists becoming a real force.

At the time this photo was taken bicycles were just coming into vogue, but compared with modern cycles were machines of torture. Before then there were a few machines mainly bone-shakers, very crude in design with wooden spokes in the wheels and penny-farthings with tyres of solid rubber, built very high and mounted from a step at the rear wheel. A speed of 10 mph was considered wonderful as the roads were not quite 'billiard table' surface.

223. The Potash during the 1800s

All traces of these cottages have long since disappeared. They stood at the junction of the Pebmarsh road with the Cangle, the lane once known as King William Street. When they became uninhabited is unknown but thought to be in the early 1920s. The name probably stemmed from the one time cottage industry of potash making, that once thrived in the county to satisfy the demand for it in the soap making and water softening industries before the 19th century. Wood, hedge cuttings, weeds and general vegetable waste was burnt and the resulting ash was then percolated in large iron pots - from where the name comes. The "lye" or remaining liquid was put in a cask into which straw was dipped, then placed over a smouldering hearth or iron pot until dry, leaving a hard crusty black potash. This was broken up and put into bags to be sold. The growth of the chemical industry saw the decline in potash making as chemical substitutes were then used. It is said too, that housewives used to save the wood ash from their fires to sell to the potash makers for a few pence to help towards their household budget. This practice also declined by the early 19th century when the growth of the coal industry lessened the use of wood resulting in this cottage industry remaining in name only. Further along this lane, on land between the Cangle and Paddy Crow is an area where the plague victims are thought to have been buried. At one time there was a Pest House in the vicinity that by the 1860s had been converted into homes for two families.

224. Halstead Cricket team, 1934

Halstead Cricket Club was formed in 1885 although the game had been played for many years before. At first the club found it difficult to find a pitch and played its matches at Earls Colne. The first match to be played at Star Stile did not take place until the 1894 season, when the pitch was a small fenced off area in the corner of Morton's Meadow. The pavilion was a large shed which also served as a store and changing rooms. Teas, cakes and bread & butter at one penny (½p) per item were served from the side under a shutter supported on two poles. This continued until 1929/30 when an attractive thatched pavilion was erected after the ground was enlarged, making the whole area very picturesque. It is said that the local gentry ran most of the entertainments in the town, arranging Sunday School treats, garden parties, musical and choral events plus bridge parties. The cricket club was very active but in its early days the working classes were mainly excluded as they could not afford the expensive gear and tended to play football instead. Recently the ground has had a face-lift with a new clubhouse being built with the aid of money from the Lottery.

The team of 1934 was from left to right:

Standing - Cyril Smith, scorer, G. Gibson, Watson Brough, Harry Clark, John Reynolds, Charles Wright, Rev C.D.N. Evans and John Pudney, umpire.

Sitting - Wilfrid D. Lougher-Goodey, Frank Reed, T. Guy N. Franklin, B.W. Basham and Jim Goodey.

225. Bois Hall in the 1800s

I was fortunate to find an old glass negative in a box, it looked interesting so I decided to have it printed. To my delight this lovely large house in the Winter's snow was revealed - a very early photo of Bois Hall. Foundations of an earlier manor house were found but this one was built about 1605, the date found on the lead drainpipes. Over the years many alterations were carried out, then in 1800 it was the victim of a disastrous fire, a common occurrence in the early days. Worse was to come in the late 1960s when demolition took place and Bois Hall Gardens developed on the site. All that remained were some mature trees, including the one in the centre of the photo but sadly this was removed a few years ago. During the 1730s Mr Sanderson Miller brought Mrs Anne Nugent, of Gosfield Hall, to Halstead and whilst she visited friends he took a walk up the Sudbury road. In a letter to Lord Dacre he describes how he saw an old house (Bois Hall) which he thought looked like the remains of an old seat. He asked to see inside and in a room where a farmer kept his corn he saw a curious chimney piece. He described his find to Mrs Nugent who wrote to Lord Tylney, the owner, to ask if she could have it if he had no need for it and she would replace it with a marble one. Lord Tylney agreed with her suggestion so the object was removed to Gosfield Hall's library. In 1748, Horace Walpole wrote to George Montague describing the library in Gosfield Hall, the seat of Nugent. He was most impressed by the chimney piece, saying it was of white alabaster, depicting the Battle of Bosworth Field with all 24 chiefs on horseback. Just the helmets and trappings of each one was gilded and the shields properly blazoned with the Arms of all of them engaged in the battle which Mrs Nugent had had restored. It was intended as a compliment to Henry VII because on either side of the chimney were the full length figures of King Henry and his queen Elizabeth, exactly resembling those on a monument in Westminster Abbey. Anne was the second wife of Robert Nugent when they married in 1736 and lived at Gosfield Hall until her death in 1756. Robert remarried the following year and was created Earl Nugent in 1776. The chimney piece is no longer at Gosfield and it is believed to have been removed to Stowe by the Marquis of Buckingham.

226. A former Straw Plait centre at 11 Sudbury Road

When the wool trade in Essex was badly hit, the Marquis of Buckingham, who lived at Gosfield Hall, introduced the art of strawplaiting in 1790 and to encourage it, the Marquis and his wife wore strawplait hats. Within a few years the industry had taken root and by the mid 1800s was giving employment to hundreds of women and children in Halstead and surrounding villages. Varieties of plait were known as The Brilliant, the finest example of local work, The Single plait, The Twistedge, and Plain Double, the latter made mainly by children and beginners. The plaiting was extensively carried on in cottages and produced a large amount of money in poor areas, though many blamed it for much idle gossip and slovenly housework. In the Summer, groups of women could be seen on village greens, on their doorsteps or under shady trees but in Winter and bad weather the work was done indoors. There were a number of buyers in the area and two of them were Alfred and Thomas Lindsell. Alfred resided at The Firs, now Dunniemead, 11 Sudbury Road, which had a large plait warehouse adjoining, now demolished but at one time after the demise of the industry, was made into a picturesque little dwelling. Alfred left Halstead in the1870s to take up residence at Luton, centre of the straw hat industry. Another dealer William Simmons set up a collection centre in Head Street at this time, but the industry started to decline. First due to foreign competition, the first plait coming from China and sold very cheaply. As time went by there was a demand for new patterns but workers were reluctant to change their methods and by 1900 strawplaiting was dead. In 1917 William tried to revive the old industry, without success as he died shortly after.

TIDINGS HILL

227. G.E. Cook's delivery vans, c1924

George Ernest Cook was the eldest son of George Cook, a brewer at the old Maltings in Parsonage Street, who in 1895 decided to branch out on his own. He acquired an off-licence on Tidings Hill, on a site that became the brewery. At first he filled one and two gallon stone jars with beer brewed by his father and delivered them to houses in a wheelbarrow, progressing later to a horse and cart. Brewing started in 1908, followed five years later by a mineral works. As the business grew a solid-tyred Maxwell motor vehicle was purchased, the body being built at Greenstead Green by Firmin's, wheelwrights. Five more vans increased the fleet for delivering to a wider area including parts of Suffolk, replacing three horse-drawn carts. A decision was made to branch out into other alcoholic drinks so a spirit and wine licence was obtained in 1926. Ralph, Ronald, Morton and George, the four eldest sons of George Ernest carried on the business after his death in 1934, with more family members joining in later years. After the war, during which beers were supplied to the forces, an off-licence was opened in the High Street in 1946, now Unwins. The brewery ceased production in 1974 and demolished 2003. The photo was taken in the mid 1920s of two of the delivery vans, with Harry Root (left), Alf Catley and Morton "Dink" Cook. An earlier brewhouse stood on Tidings Hill near the Rayner Way entrance, close by a beerhouse called The Fox run by Lydia Wright and her son Ben until 1862, when the premises were sold. Beer continued to be sold by William Deal, followed by Henry Corder, a beer retailer during the first three decades of the 1900s.

228. Tidings Hill in the early 1900s

An early view of Tidings Hill pictures all the neatly fenced gardens that have gradually given way to the car. About a century ago most people walked everywhere and it is fitting that a walking-stick maker lived on the hill. Alfred Pamplin, one of 13 children, came to Halstead with his family and lived at 1 Tidings Hill for more than 50 years. At the end of the garden stands a small brick built house, thought to have been a weaving shop in the early 1800s. This is where Alfred manufactured walking-sticks, the business he took over from his father, John. He used to walk round the countryside looking for suitable wild rose branches, which he cut and seasoned. His sticks were sold to London businesses and used by many famous people including KingGeorge V and in 1924 he was awarded the freedom of the City of London. Alf's son, Karl, educated at Earls Colne Grammar School, had the distinction of being the first Mayor of the London Borough of Barnet in 1965.

During World War II ghostly happenings caused concern on the hill one night during the blackout, when the sound of clanking chains was heard and a white shape was seen coming down the hill. Soldiers camped in Raven's Meadow were put on alert and the police were summoned. Fear turned to laughter when the 'ghost' was caught - a large white goat had broken free from its tether at the side of the road near Stone's Farm and decided to go walkabout, dragging a length of chain behind it. During the late 1800s and early 1900s fish and chips were fried in a tin shed on the allotments down School Lane between Tidings Hill and Mitchell Avenue because frying in the town was forbidden. The birds did not complain as they flocked in their hundreds to fight over the scraps.

TRINITY ROAD

229. Owen Terrace, Trinity Road, c1900

In 1890 it was decided by the Halstead Industrial Co-operative Society to erect a pair of cottages in Trinity Road at a cost of £265. One was soon bought for £180 so it was decided to carry on and build a total of eighteen, and due to a ready demand they were quickly sold. Owen Terrace was named after Robert Owen, a great Co-operative pioneer, and were the first examples of decent homes for the working classes. They were all fronted by a low wall surmounted by attractive iron railings with an iron gate. The fences were removed for scrap during World War II.

230. The Co-op premises, Trinity Street, c1900

Halstead Industrial Co-operative Society Ltd was formed in 1860 and four years later some premises were purchased in Trinity Street, on the corner of Rosemary Lane, where necessary changes were made and five cottages built at the rear. This ornate building was erected, partly on the site of the old one in 1887, complete with the beehive emblem in the brickwork. In later years the old building to the left was obtained for a butchery and shoe shop. A decision was made in 1923 to extend the larger building making it similar to how we see it today, with another small extension added in 1957. To commemorate the 75th anniversary of the Branch in 1935, a clock was erected and being situated near the bus and railway stations and local industries, proved to be invaluable and was sorely missed when rust set in causing its removal in 1970. The gap between the two buildings was the entrance to the Working Men's Club, then a room in Rosemary Lane behind the Co-op. Rosemary Lane, the home of the foundry, gasworks and situated beside the railway, all producing a lot of dirt, seemed to have been misnamed. The lane is very old and before the 1700s was called Pritchards Lane after a house, held in the past by a family of that name. The lane originally took a left turn near the present day Chapel Street junction and led straight across to Slough Farm. It was formerly a watercourse, but many years ago the tenant at the farm decided that he wanted a nearer approach to the town than going round Chapel Hill, so he filled in the watercourse to make a roadway leading to Rosemary Lane and referred to as The Common. The coming of the railway and the Beridge/Stanley Road development altered it. Before the 20th century little cottages lined the lane behind the Co-op but five were pulled down in 1915 on account of their insanitary condition. About 1949, two more were converted by the Co-op into a well-equipped miniature ice-cream factory. Unfortunately the demand for wafers and cornets changed to blocks and choc ices which the Society was unable to supply and was defeated by the larger producers. By 1955 all the remaining dwellings were converted into Co-op warehousing.

231. The Trinity Street level crossing in the 1950s

This photo taken in the 1950s shows the railway level crossing, subject of many a row and lots of tempers being lost, when the gates were closed to traffic and pedestrians. Foundry and factory workers would get very irate, especially if they were going home for a meal and their time was limited. On one occasion a long excursion train stood across Trinity Street whilst 350 people scrambled aboard. A large crowd soon gathered, became impatient and jumped over the gates and ran round the carriages, but they were not the only ones to get annoyed - several workers from Hedingham could not get out of the train due to its length and the absence of corridors and were consequently taken on to Colne station. All this became a thing of the past when the railway finally closed in April 1965.

A W.H. Smith bookstall was opened at Haverhill in 1888 but it was not until 1899 that a branch was opened at Halstead. During those 11 years a local lad, H. Iron, travelled on the early morning train with the guard to meet the newspaper train from London at Marks Tey. On his return journey he sorted the papers to deliver when he reached Halstead. The guard used to send him to Marks Tey on his own complaining he did not feel well but on return he was seen to emerge from the Railway Tavern outside Chappel Station saying he felt much better. From a lad on the Colne Valley line collecting papers for W.H. Smith, he was appointed to Liverpool Street main bookstall. On retirement in 1946 he had completed 57 years with the company. The station yard became the bus park in 1950 and a new bookstall was erected in the corner (left).

232. Trinity Street on a postcard dated 1905

You are now standing on the level crossing looking along the row of little shops in Trinity Street before 1905. The last two-storey building was the old Railway Bell, formerly the Bell, but gained an extra word when the railway came to town in 1860. For many years this hostelry was a landmark in Trinity Street where thirsty people called for a warmer in the cold weather or a cooler in the Summer. It was boarded up after its closure in 1907, becoming an eyesore. Eventually demolition took place in 1913 to make way for a Picture Palace. It was a surprise that it stood the test of time as huge timber beams built into the chimneys were well roasted and charred. The Colne Valley Cinema opened in 1916 and later took the name of the Savoy, closing in 1963, to be a Chinese takeaway. Doubledays, Trinity branch, on the right, closed in 1916 due to the difficulty in obtaining assistants during hostilities. Another pub The Two Brewers once stood on the site of 24 Trinity Street.

233. Trinity Street/Kings Road junction, c1964

An historic event took place here on April 12th 1928. After the coming of the motor car, the wireless, the airplane and the cinema in the previous decades, Halstead witnessed the coming of electricity. Among flags, bunting and streamers decorating the area were a number of bulbs, which lit up when Mr E.B. Parker, chairman of the Halstead Urban District Council, switched on the electricity supply to the town at the kiosk by the park gate. Another kiosk where power was transformed was situated near the library in Colchester Road (61). The photo shows the Railway Goods yard entrance with an advertising hoarding in the corner, now the petrol station.

A terrible fatality took place in this vicinity on May 31st 1914, when a horse bolted, with a cart, from outside the Three Pigeons whilst unattended. It raced down Mount Hill at a terrific speed after all attempts to stop it failed. In Trinity Street Mrs Amy Portway, unaware of what was happening as she rode her cycle with an attached auto-wheel, was overtaken by the horse but the cart struck her and threw her heavily to the ground. She was picked up and taken into the Temperance Hotel (234), outside where the accident occurred. Three local doctors were quickly on the scene but as her injuries were so serious a specialist was fetched from London by Harry Cooper. An operation was performed at her home, Bois Hall (225) but sadly she passed away the following day. The horse was eventually caught after it smashed into the level crossing gates, closed for an approaching train.

234. Trinity Street, c1900

This early view, looking down Trinity Street, shows two large neatly fenced houses on the left, which were converted into the offices of Holmes and Hills. The adjoining house, No. 38, became the Halstead Gazette office in March 1967, a few doors away from the old office in the Caxton Works, up Hall Yard beside the neighbouring Temperance Hotel. A draper's shop and two cottages were burnt down in the 1870s and the hotel built on the site. After the opening of the Temperance Hall, later Hotel, there was an invitation to proceed to the Howe, home of Mrs Hornor. The party set off in an omnibus during a terrible snowstorm, and on reaching the Workhouse (111) encountered a 10ft snowdrift. It took the guests an hour just to walk to the Howe (118), as the force of the wind had brought down many trees. Carriages of the train coming from Hedingham were also said to have been lifted up. Halstead Working Men's Club was formed in the new Temperance Hall on March 21st 1877 where it stayed for two years. Due to the rules of no intoxicating drinks or gambling, the club moved to Rosemary Lane in a room rented from the Co-op. These premises became too cramped so in 1923 the club acquired some premises in Trinity Square (Butler Road) but before they could move Portways built an extension to the Rosemary Lane clubroom where it remained until returning to the old Temperance Hotel in 1979. The membership stood at 800 but during the ensuing years this fell to 80, bringing financial difficulties, forcing the club to close its doors in 1986 after 109 years. The former hotel was then converted into flats.

235. The Public Gardens in 1902

A committee was formed in the town during 1897 to decide in what form the Diamond Jubilee of Queen Victoria could be marked. Various schemes were put forward and with George Courtauld's £1,000 and other public donations, it was decided to provide a recreation ground. Areas suggested were - the land which later became Pretoria Road, the allotments opposite the hospital, the meadow, now the Broton Estate and the area that was chosen. The decision caused many arguments as it was allotments from which rents benefited local schools under the Will of William Martin. A public meeting was called at which a poll was taken, resulting in this location being favoured. On Whit Monday 1901, Alfred Kibble, chairman of the ground committee, handed George Courtauld the key to unlock the main gate and open the grounds to the public. The groundwork was supervised by Alfred Fairbank to the plans of T.W. Saunders, editor of Amateur Gardening. The bandstand was made and donated by Charles Portway along with a drinking fountain. Twelve seats were given and the pond supplied with water from the Mount Well, a connection being made with Adams' brewery pipe. Iron fencing round the boundary was installed making a huge improvement to the area. Instead of an untidy field, with a lot of lumber and a ragged hedge, there was a broad path with a fence and a row of beautiful horse chestnut trees lining the road, donated by Mr Adams. Shelters were added a decade later. After accidents occurred to bullocks being impaled on the spiked fence Portway's foundry produced hundreds of small iron balls in 1930, which were fixed on the spikes - some can still be seen today in front of the Community Centre. The gnarled apple tree in the centre of the photo, was a remnant of the old orchard and was chopped down shortly after when young lads climbed over the fence to 'scrump' the fruit. The row of horse chestnuts were all felled in 1971 after one toppled on a passing vehicle one foggy day.

236. Brewery workers, c1877

Thomas Francis Adams worked for the City of London Brewery for 26 years, where his son Edgar joined him in 1869. They both paid a visit to the Halstead brewery of Stanton Grey & Co. of which they ultimately became the owners in September 1876. On leaving London the family took up residence at Red House, Colchester Road (64) and made many improvements to the brewery. This group photo was probably taken to record the erection of the clock tower on top of the brewery building in 1877. Thomas, who died the following year after an accident, is seen here on the right, with his sons Edgar and Percy, posing with the workers. In 1939 the brewery was sold to Isherwood, Foster and Stacey, a subsidiary of Fremlin's, although the Adams family retained the Brewery Chapel (238), adjacent cottage, mineral water business and rights to supply malt. The site was bought in 1965 and converted into the Halstead Urban District Council offices and yard. The building spanning the yard was demolished and the clock found a new home on top of the bandstand in the park during 1971, where it remained until a 'facelift' to the park saw its demise.

237. Mr E.T. Adams outside the Brewery, c1910

Here we see Edgar Tarry Adams posing beside his bottle-shaped car, surrounded by inquisitive young lads outside the Brewery circa 1910. Edgar came to Halstead in 1876 and resided with his family at Red House, Colchester Road (64). He married in 1880 and moved to The Cottage (left), which had just been rebuilt on the site of a large old house. The Cottage was purchased by the local council in 1965 and converted into offices, opened in October 1966 - now the Braintree District Council Office, Trinity Street. Between the garden walls of Trinity House and Holmes and Hills you can see an entrance leading to Adam's Court and the Coach House. This building was opened in 1910 as a mineral works attached to the Adam's brewery, where soda water, ginger beer and lemonade were made and bottled - said to have exceptional nice flavours.

One member of the Adams' staff was Walter Cocksedge, who completed 56½ years service at the brewery. He was the rent collector and with a top-hatted coachman rode around all the pubs owned by Adams in the town and surrounding countryside, about 40 in total, collecting the money due.

238. Adams Brewery Chapel

Thomas Adams' death led his sons to build a chapel at the brewery as a memorial to him in 1883, with a dual purpose of both chapel and reading-room, to promote religion and learning for the workers. The chapel was open two evenings during the week as a reading-room and a short service was conducted on Sunday afternoons for the workmen and their families. The Church of All Hallows the Great, rebuilt by Christopher Wren after the Great Fire of London, stood next door to the City of London Brewery in Thames Street, where the Adams' had worked. In 1896 this church was demolished and some of the fittings found their way to Halstead. These probably inspired the present brickbuilt chapel to be reconstructed in 1902 as a memorial to Thomas and Mary Adams. Percy was an accomplished organist and Edgar a lay preacher and chaplain to the Workhouse and they conducted the services previously held in a corner of the Granary. The reredos, pillars and archway with cherub still remain in the chapel, the 17th century font was taken to the Chapel Royal at Hampton Court Palace after World War II, the stained glass from the Chancel windows is at the RAF Chapel at Hendon and the organ is in New Street Methodist Church (190). The Bung Chapel, as it is affectionately known, was once a busy meeting place but stood derelict for years and became surrounded by Adam's Court. Halstead & District Local History Society were looking for suitable premises and after negotiations opened a museum on August 17th 1985 but this has since closed due to lack of support.

239. Halstead's Police Station in the early 1900s

Halstead's gaol (20) was sold for £750 and the proceeds paid for the building of a new Police Station in Trinity Street, then Chapel Street, in 1850. An article written in the 1930s, by a local historian, says that a John Sewell lived in a house situated near the site, more than a century before, and grew large quantities of lavender, hops and saffron. His son was the founder of the brewery opposite which later became Adams Brewery (236). John was a descendant of another John Sewell, of Henny Mill, who introduced the Bay & Say trade to Halstead in 1470. Saffron was grown for the dye it produced, being used also in perfumes, flavourings for cakes and medicines. The market declined with the Bay trade and by 1790 had disappeared entirely. An old Halsteadian could remember Dr John Cornelius Taylor living in the old house called Chapel House (190), who had a very large garden and orchard where he planted many acres of lavender. This was gathered by women and children in season, for him to make lavender oil in his distillery, part of which was made into lavender water. The photo was taken in the early 1900s of the station and adjoining police house. It was the first purpose built station provided for the Essex County Constabulary and had two cells. The station was extended after the inspector moved to a new house further up the road about 1960, when the surrounding garden and fences were removed to make way for the cars that took over from bicycles and officers on foot.

240. Holy Trinity School choir, 1954

Holy Trinity Upper National School was erected in 1845 with just two classrooms of flint construction. Over the years additions were made and modernisation has brought it up to the standard we see today. Tidings Hill School was opened in 1858 in School Chase as an auxiliary to Holy Trinity, for the convenience of pupils living in that area and originally consisted of just one room for 66 children. In 1905 a decision was made to transfer all the 11-year-olds to Holy Trinity but after five years the school was closed altogether and converted into two cottages. The photo records the School choir of 1954.

Back Row, left to right : David Bayley, Tony O'Connell, Graham Britton, Roger Cook, Brian Hart, Johnny Boreham, Peter Sach and Neil Darnell.

Middle Row : Mary Rawdon, Elizabeth Evans, Linda Warren, Susan Cowling, Joy Wicker, Carole Warren, Brenda Arnold, Susan Root, Joy Ruggles and Susan Allin.

Front Row : Maureen Argent, Lorraine Smith, Susan Redgewell, Jennifer Juniper, Janet Suckling, Miss Gertrude Dewing, Sylvia Rayner, Margaret Hunwicks, Pat Hasler, Sheila Harding, Gloria Bearham and Janice Juniper.

241. The Police Barracks in Trinity Street, c1900

The county buildings in Trinity Street were erected in 1865, to serve as barracks for a sergeant and two constables in the Police Force. In 1881 twelve people were living here including five police constables. The barracks were considered unsuitable for occupation and demolished in 1959 when a detached house was built on the site for the Inspector, using bricks salvaged from the old barracks. It is now a private residence aptly named Barrack House. The barracks, Trinity Terrace and the Police Station were all built on part of the Chapel House estate. Somewhere in this vicinity was a large eight bed-roomed house that Courtaulds rented, opening it in November 1849 as a Factory Home for the benefit of single female workers of good character. The aim was to give them a better life away from the evils of over-crowded cottages and common lodging houses, where often women "particularly adverse to morality" took in girls, many from the rural areas and led them astray. Many were opposed to this plan as they would lose the lodgers whose money helped to pay the rent. The Home was a pleasant place with a coach-house and stables. There was a flower and kitchen garden where the girls were allowed to pass the time. Rules were very strict and had to be obeyed. The bedrooms contained two to five single beds and each lodger had to make her bed and vacate the room by 9 in the morning, returning no earlier than 8 but before 10 at night. There was a long dining-room and a large sitting room. The house-keeper, a strong middle-aged servant had her room by the door - no doubt checking that the rules were adhered to. Mary Merryweather, who was in charge, had rooms at the garden end of the house, separated from but in easy reach of the girls who paid 1/- (5p) per week for their lodgings, including washing. The Home, an experiment lasted seven years during which time 67 girls took advantage of the establishment, with one girl resident for the whole duration.

242. White Ash Green

This area contains a lot of local history, thanks to Robert Lock. The post supporting the White Ash Green sign started life in Colchester Road displaying the King's Head sign (46), and was saved to be erected on the corner at the Halstead side of the hamlet. Beside the sign is a seat built with bricks, most of which were made in old local brickyards and collected over the years by Robert Lock and Chips Allen. One special brick commemorating the marriage of Prince Charles and Lady Diana Spencer on July 29th 1981 was donated by the late Kay Allen. The seat bears the names of all the residents living in White Ash Green at the new Millennium and was erected by a local man, the late John Stubbings.

243. Windmill Road children, 1948

The Council wished to acquire a piece of land for the development of Windmill Road in 1929. Negotiations were made to purchase land from two owners, but there was no access as Mr Vaizey reserved the existing right of way for Blamster's Farmhouse. Fortunately Mrs Lightfoot, wife of the Methodist minister, offered to sell part of her Rose Cottage (35) garden to provide an entrance from Chapel Hill. The name originated from the fact that a windmill formerly stood in the field off Mount Hill and was burnt down with two cottages after being struck by lightning in August 1800. In 1946, twenty prefabricated houses were erected at the top of Windmill Road to alleviate the housing shortage after the war, serving a useful purpose until 1967 when Spansey Court occupied the site. In 1945 an American serviceman parked his jeep in the road on trips to the town. He soon made friends with the children, who called him "King". He promised that he would return one day and kept his word. Arthur Gustafson of Connecticut returned in August 1948, bringing presents for all the Windmill Road children. During the war he was stationed at Gosfield with the 397th Bomb Group of the 9th US Airforce and is seen here giving out gifts to Margaret Wright and other children before taking them all to the cinema.

244. John Bragg

Now you have strolled round the town, I hope your shoes are not in the same state as the ones presenting a problem for John Bragg. James Tyler, who had a studio at Oakleigh House, Upper Chapel Street, photographed John in 1896 and won a front page exhibition in the Christian Herald and a trophy. John Bragg did not lead a tranquil life among the soles and heels as might be suggested by the photo. He was a cobbler, but was also one of the town's most off-beat characters. Once, jailed for poaching, he was sent to Chelmsford Prison. Within a short time he had locked up his warder, walked from Chelmsford to Halstead and on arriving in the town, swam two miles along the River Colne, to escape the advancing local constabulary. No one seemed to know whether or not he was intercepted, but later years found him in the water again. For some time he was attendant at the old Bathing Place (39). Even though he was in his seventies, he saved the lives of no less than thirteen people and was awarded a diploma by the Royal Humane Society and a silver medal by his colleagues when one afternoon in 1895 he emerged from the pool with a small boy under each arm. At Guy Fawkes, every year he went about the town with a guy, working furiously to raise money for charitable institutions. Someone suggested that he probably had an admiration for Mr Fawkes' principles. This grand old man passed away in 1905. Another man named Bragg - George, known as 'Rocky', followed in his footsteps and also paraded around the town with a guy collecting money for the hospital. He was also the Town Crier and died in 1937.

Some memories of two Halsteadians of the mid 1800s

These memories were recalled by William Drury in 1925 aged 95 years. Going back some 80 years William recalled something of the conditions under which men lived and laboured. For instance, at the age of eight, when most youngsters have just begun to realise that they have entered school for serious purposes, he was already working, and his hours were from daylight till dark, whatever times that meant. For this, he received the sum of 2d (1p) per day, and from his memories of those days, there is little reason to think that he considered himself underpaid! The men with whom he worked on the land had the same hours for 9/- (45p) per week. His own father worked for this wage, having to support his wife, five sons and three daughters. The place where he put in his many hours for 2d per day was a large garden which existed on the site of the Railway Station (210) then owned by William Cook (103). Later, he went as stockman to Mr Emberson of Sloe House, where his wages increased to 9/- (45p) per week.

Naturally feeding was a serious problem on a wage like this and it is interesting to know what his mother did to fill the mouths of her family. Her main food supply was potatoes and when times were good she would buy a piece of the fattest pork obtainable for 1/- (5p), melt down the pork into dripping, cook the potatoes then pour the fat all over them, so making what the children considered to be a very special dish. Bread at that time was 1/- (5p) per loaf and a quarter ounce of tea cost 3d (1½p) and that had to make several brews. As for pudding the children were very fortunate if they had any at all. At that time half a pound of rice could be purchased for 1d (½p) which would be boiled for a little time until soft, mixed with a little flour to make it solid and sprinkled with sugar - a mark of really good times.

The early days of the workhouse was well remembered by William who played on the ground before the workhouse was built in Hedingham Road (111). It was erected to house the poor in the Winter when they had nothing to do - a common experience of all land workers in those days. There was no kind of work carried on in the workhouse, but the inmates were herded there, roughly fed and sent out periodically to look for work. In 1881, William entered a comfortable period of his life when he became coachman and gardener to Mr Portway, a post in which he stayed for 32 years until his employer's death. He did not retire at that time and was still working at the age of 95 years. He had never had a day's holiday, being far too busy looking for some sort of living. He married at 20 years old and brought up four children.

He remembered the time when local landowners and farmers decided that labour was too well paid and held a meeting with the intention of keeping men off the land till they would take less money. Many of the men thus cast out of employment never returned, being shipped to Canada and other Colonies where they stayed.

William Drury was a working class man who lived in Box Mill Lane and by contrast the following memories were recalled by Mrs Alice Vaizey, daughter of Mr & Mrs Hornor of the Howe (118), who after her marriage spent many years at Attwoods.

Most of her long life was spent in prominent association with all social and other movements which had Halstead and its neighbours as their centre. In the days spent at the Howe with her parents, brothers and sisters, there were no facilities for travel and the smallest journey was a matter for serious consideration as an undertaking. As a result no one left home other than on a very special occasion, finding their pleasure in their own family circle. There were many people in Halstead who had never seen the sea and knew nothing of how the outside world progressed.

In those days there were two annual fairs, one in October, the other in April. These were held on the Market Hill, where at that time there was no fountain and the horse-drawn caravans reached from the top to the bottom of the hill. She remembered the Menageries and had vivid recollections of November 5th. A very large bonfire was formed on the top of the Market Hill and one of the favourite sports was to light tar barrels then roll them down the street.

The quietness of the life of those days was emphasised by the fact that there were no evening entertainments, but her father, in connection with other local gentlemen, was instrumental in getting up the "Penny Readings", which for a few years were a popular feature of the town's life. These took the form of readings from Shakespeare and poetry, with occasional singing for which there was a charge of one penny. Some youngsters only cared for the comical ones and were easily bored. Instead of listening, boys would pull girls' hair in front of them or let mice loose. At one event at the Town Hall all the gaslights went out - some youths had entered the rear of the building and blown down the gas pipe resulting in pandemonium. "Spelling Bees" were also popular - a large number of people ascended the platform and words were given them to spell. All who could not do this had to go back to their seats and the last to remain on the platform was the winner. Occasional lectures were given and she specially remembered one given by a man who escaped from slavery.

She recalled that there was not a sweet shop in the town and the only source of supply could be obtained from a Mrs Toby Wicker, who kept a fishmonger's shop at 67 High Street. It was customary for the boot & shoemaker, also the tailor to visit the Howe to take measurements and instructions. There was a Miss Firmin who had a select millinery business at Broomhill, Colchester Road.

Mrs Vaizey recalled the fact that the one holiday of the year in her younger days was the Flower Show, organised by Halstead people but held at various large estates in the neighbourhood, such as Stisted Hall, Gosfield Hall etc. most of the population left the town for that day to attend, all the shops were shut for the day, everyone had new clothes as far as possible and altogether the Show was the event of the year.

Her recollections of the movements leading to the founding of the Greenwood School are of interest. Before its establishment in which Lucy Greenwood (176) was materially assisted by Mr Hornor, the old part of the school was a Smallpox Hospital, which her father regularly visited. Fear of infection was unknown to him, for he would return to his home after these visits without even a change of clothes.

The front part overlooking Head Street (92), was subsequently built and used for the St Andrew's Schools. When Lucy wished to purchase these buildings for the establishment of the Industrial School, John T. Adams of Firwoods, built the St Andrew's Schools in Colchester Road (57). Girls of her younger days were not commonly supposed to need much education, but she could remember a school for girls run by a Miss Nott in a very old house in Colchester Road, (this is now the Chinese takeaway). About 20 girls attended this school and every year they visited the Howe (118) for their annual picnic, wearing their bonnets and sandals - a custom of the school.

Mrs Vaizey recalled the time when Canon Ingles, vicar of St Andrew's, decided to remove the choir to the East end of the church. Those members who were in the habit of sitting in the chancel were allocated seats in the nave of the church. One local gentleman habitually used two seats, one for himself and the other for his large hat and was so annoyed when it was impossible for him to have the use of both seats that he left the church forever, resisting all persuasion to return.

Mrs Vaizey remembered the time that the steam threshing machine was introduced into the neighbourhood, an action that enraged the workers so much that a special guard had to watch over the machinery to protect it from damage. Her reminiscences went back to before the days of the Colne Valley Railway when the nearest station was at Braintree. Her first trip to Clacton was undertaken when a horse-drawn bus carried passengers to Braintree to board a train as far as Weeley from where the remainder of the journey was either riding or driving by horse.

The memories of these two people from very different backgrounds give us some idea of what life was like in the mid 1800s and it is due to The Halstead Gazette for recording them nearly a century ago that we can have "A look back at Halstead".

Halstead & District Local History Society

(Registered Charity No. 289304)

PUBLICATIONS PRICE LIST

The following are the only books still available

No.	Title	Price	P & P Extra
4	**Discover Halstead** - 3rd Edition - an Historic Guide by P.A.L. Bamberger	£4.50	£1.00
5	**Halstead & Colne Valley at War (1939-1945)** by Dave Osborne	£4.50	£1.00
6	**A Centenary History of Halstead Hospital (1884-1984)** by Adrian Corder-Birch	£1.95	£1.00
7	**Vintage Steam Owners and Operators of the Colne Valley Area** by Robin A. Harding	£2.75	£1.00
8	**Schools and Scholars in Halstead and District** by Mary Downey and Doreen Potts	£2.50	£1.00
9	**Halstead and the Urban District Council (1894-1974)** by Geoffrey Copsey	£2.00	£1.00
11	**A Pictorial History of Sible Hedingham** by Adrian Corder-Birch	£4.75	£1.00
12	**Halstead's Heritage** by Doreen Potts	£4.95	£1.00
13	**From Construction to Destruction - An Authentic History of the Colne Valley & Halstead Railway** by E.P. Willingham	£12.50	£3.00
14	**Pictures from the Past - Castle Hedingham in Old Photographs** by Charles James Bird	£3.50	£1.00
15	**The History of Law and Order in North Hinkford (North East Essex)** by F.W. Pawsey	£9.95	£1.50
16	**Time Was - Childhood Memories of the Maplesteads** by M.J. Aldous	£4.50	£1.00
17	**People at Work in Halstead and District** by Doreen Potts	£5.50	£1.00
18	**Great Yeldham** by Adrian Corder-Birch	£6.95	£1.75
19	**Hunt for Machinery** by P.J. Burton-Hopkins	£6.95	£1.75
20	**Snapshots. An Essex Village Childhood 1929-1945** *(about Bulmer)* by Bob Hawksley	£6.95	£1.50

Postal orders for the above books should be sent to:-
Jim Hutchins, 6 Stone Cottages, Greenstead Green, Halstead, Essex, CO9 1QT
Telephone 01787 472511
Cheques, in English pounds sterling, payable to Halstead & District Local History Society

INDEX

C

D

I

J

K

L

M

N

O

P

Q

R

S

T

U

V

W

Y